THE STRANGE STORY
OF
ADA GOODRICH FREER

BY TREVOR H. HALL

BIBLIOGRAPHY

A Bibliography of Books on Conjuring in English from 1580 to 1850
Mathematical Recreations (1633): An Exercise in Seventeenth Century Bibliography
Old Conjuring Books: A Bibliographical and Historical Study
The Winder Sale of Old Conjuring Books
Some Printers and Publishers of Conjuring Books and other Ephemera, 1800—1850 (with Percy H. Muir)

SHERLOCK HOLMES

Sherlock Holmes. Ten Literary Studies
The Late Mr. Sherlock Holmes
Sherlock Holmes. The Higher Criticism
Sherlock Holmes and His Creator

DOROTHY L. SAYERS

Dorothy L. Sayers. Nine Literary Studies

CRITICAL PSYCHICAL RESEARCH

The Haunting of Borley Rectory: A Critical Survey of the Evidence
(with E. J. Dingwall and K. M. Goldney)
The Strange Case of Edmund Gurney
New Light on Old Ghosts
The Spiritualists: The Story of William Crookes and Florence Cook
The Strange Story of Ada Goodrich Freer
(first published as part of *Strange Things* by T. H. H. with J. L. Campbell)

CONJURING

The Testament of R. W. Hull
Nothing is Impossible
Reading is Believing
The Card Magic of Edward G. Brown

HISTORICAL INVESTIGATION

The Early Years of the Huddersfield Building Society
The Mystery of the Leeds Library
Search for Harry Price

'Miss X' November 1894. The only photograph of Ada Goodrich Freer in the files of the Society for Psychical Research, by whose courtesy this copy is reproduced.

The Strange Story of
Ada Goodrich Freer

TREVOR H. HALL
M.A., Ph.D., F.S.A.

With an Introduction by
ELIOT SLATER
C.B.E., M.D., LL.D.

DUCKWORTH

First published in this edition in 1980 by
Gerald Duckworth & Co. Ltd.
The Old Piano Factory
43 Gloucester Crescent
London NW1

First published as part of *Strange Things*
by J. L. Campbell and T. H. Hall
(Routledge and Kegan Paul, 1968)

ISBN 0 7156 1427 4

British Library Cataloguing in Publication Data

Hall, Trevor Henry
    The strange story of Ada Goodrich Freer.
    1. Freer, Ada Goodrich
    2. Psychical research - Great Britain - Biography
    1. Title
    133.9′092′4   BF1027.F/

ISBN 0-7156-1427-4

CONTENTS

For Marguerite

PREFACE

In 1968 *Strange Things* was published by Routledge & Kegan Paul. The collaborating authors were Dr John Lorne Campbell of Canna, the distinguished scholar well-known for his work on the Gaelic oral tradition, and myself.

Strange Things was a long book of 350 pages, and was divided into four sections, 'The Society for Psychical Research Enquiry into Second Sight in the Scottish Highlands' (eleven chapters written by Dr Campbell), 'The Strange Story of Ada Goodrich Freer' (nine chapters, written by myself), 'Ada Goodrich Freer and Fr Allan McDonald's Folklore Collection' (three chapters written by Dr Campbell) and 'Strange Things' (being broadly speaking the folk-lore collection assembled and so named by Fr Allan McDonald of Eriskay, translated and edited by Dr Campbell). In his Preface to our book, Dr Campbell wrote:

It seems desirable that something should be said of the circumstances under which this book came to be written.

When I first went to live on the island of Barra in the Outer Hebrides in 1933, many people were living who could remember Fr Allan McDonald, priest of the island of Eriskay, who had died in 1905 at the age of 46. Alike as a parish priest, a poet, and a collector of Gaelic folklore, Fr Allan McDonald had achieved a fame that lived on long after him. It therefore seemed to me extraordinary that a folklore collection as important as his should have disappeared completely. The collection seemed well worth trying to trace, and eventually, after prolonged enquiries (and in spite of the denials of two persons who actually were in possession of parts of it), I was able to trace four-fifths of it with the help of various clerical and academic friends, to whom I shall always be profoundly grateful.

The material traced consisted of eight quarto notebooks. One of these contained a collection of rare Gaelic words and expressions made in South Uist and Eriskay between 1893 and 1897; another a collection of Gaelic hymns, some traditional, some original, and some translated from English and Latin; another contained a collection of the words of waulking (labour) songs; and another, about which more will be said later, contained a collection of second sight stories and other material,

vii

including draft versions of some of Fr Allan McDonald's original Gaelic poems. Apart from these four notebooks there were four others containing general folklore—local history, folk-tales, folk-songs, folk anecdotes, proverbs, place-names, Uist and Eriskay genealogies, and so on. These were numbered I, II, V, and VI. This part of the collection had been begun in the winter of 1887–8 and had been made over the succeeding ten years. Notebooks III and IV were (and still are) missing; these had been written on Eriskay between 1893 and 1896.

An examination of the four surviving folklore notebooks and of a diary kept by Fr Allan McDonald between 1st September 1897 and 30th June 1898 revealed that a lady named Ada Goodrich Freer, well known in folklore circles as the authoress of an important book on the Hebrides called *Outer Isles*, published in 1902, and a lecturer on several occasions between 1897 and 1901 to the Folklore Society in London and other similar bodies on Hebridean folklore, had been indebted to Fr Allan McDonald's notebooks for her material to a very remarkable degree, though this was not fully realized until a catalogue of his folklore material, which was begun by myself, was completed by Miss Sheila J. Lockett, who also spent some time in checking Fr Allan McDonald's material against Miss Freer's lectures and publications for me. An outcome of this discovery was my article 'The late Fr Allan McDonald, Miss Goodrich Freer and Hebridean Folklore', published in the second volume of *Scottish Studies* in 1958 (pp. 175–88) giving examples of her indebtedness. The article had previously been rejected by several Scottish editors on the grounds that it was 'too contentious'; but the impression the exposure made at the time appears to have been minimal.[1] The present book is to a considerable extent a confirmation, and extension, of the thesis presented in that article.

The revelation that Miss Freer had been an extensive copyist of Fr Allan McDonald's folklore notebooks suggested the possibility that her literary remains, if they could be found, might well contain material copied verbatim from the two missing notebooks. But enquiries made of probable societies and institutions, including the Folklore Society, the Society for Psychical Research, and the Royal Geographical Society, of all of which Miss Freer had been a prominent member, drew a complete blank. The literary remains of Miss Freer, who had been a very well-known writer on folklore and psychical research between 1889 and 1902, authoress of many books, articles, and lectures and the person in charge of the Society for Psychical Research's enquiry into second sight in the Highlands financed by Lord Bute, in 1894, have vanished utterly. Her widowed husband, the late Rev. H. H. Spoer, then living in New York, told me by letter in 1950, the year before he died, that he and his wife had not been able to keep many papers during their travels in the Near East between 1905 and 1923, and that his wife had always returned any

---

[1] For example, an offprint of the article was sent to the editor of *Folklore*, but as far as I know the article was never mentioned in that journal.

material she borrowed to its owners. Nevertheless, it still seems very odd that no literary remains of such a well-known writer have been preserved anywhere. The possible reason for this will be suggested in due course.

It was obvious, when Fr Allan McDonald's collection was traced, that it contained much material of interest that ought to be published. Priority was given to his collection of rare words and expressions from the Gaelic dialect of South Uist and Eriskay, as this provided a very useful key to difficulties in Gaelic folk-tales and folk-songs collected in South Uist and Barra, and also in Fr Allan McDonald's own Gaelic poems. After arrangements to publish this work in Edinburgh had fallen through, it was accepted by the Dublin Institute for Advanced Studies and published in Dublin in 1958, under the title of *Gaelic Words from South Uist*. The next material chosen from Fr Allan McDonald's collection for publication was his own poems,[1] and after that, the ghost and second sight stories, which are published in this book (in the great majority of cases for the first time) and which it seemed particularly desirable should be published under circumstances which gave Fr Allan McDonald the fullest possible credit for their collection.

When preparing these for publication, it seemed to me that there would be little point in adding even such an interesting collection to the already large amount of material of this kind from the Scottish Highlands that is in print without saying something about the circumstances under which the collection had been made. This involved investigating, and writing the first complete account of, the Society for Psychical Research's enquiry into second sight in the Highlands and Islands of Scotland, which was financed by the third Marquess of Bute, begun in 1892, taken charge of by Miss Freer in the autumn of 1894, and after two interim reports from her in December 1894 and December 1895, mysteriously faded out of sight and came to nothing. In writing this account I have been most fortunate in being allowed access to the unpublished correspondence dealing with the enquiry in the third Marquess of Bute's papers.

My enquiries about Miss Freer herself and about what had happened to her literary remains came to a dead-end in 1953. It was not until 1964, when I happened to read Mr Trevor H. Hall's *The Strange Case of Edmund Gurney* (the story of the first secretary of the Society for Psychical Research, who committed suicide in mysterious circumstances in 1888, the year Miss Freer became an Associate of the Society), that I felt that here there was a person, a trained and critical investigator who was thoroughly well informed about the background to psychical research in England in the 1880s and 1890s, and about the strange personalities involved in it, who might know something about Miss Freer or could suggest how more might be discovered about her, and perhaps help to

[1] Published in 1965, with some translations by the writer, under the title *Bàrdachd Mhgr. Ailein*, T. & A. Constable, Edinburgh.

do so. I wrote to Mr Hall, and a large correspondence soon developed on the subject, turning eventually into a full and happy collaboration, in which Mr Hall undertook the writing of the account of Miss Freer's carefully concealed origin and of her peculiar and controversial career in psychical research between 1889, the date of her first address to the S.P.R., and 1901, when she left England for Jerusalem. This, too, is published here for the first time. I have been exceptionally fortunate in having Mr Hall as a collaborator, as it would have been quite impossible to write an adequate account of Miss Freer based on her career in folklore alone: it is significant that the remarks in three of Alexander Carmichael's letters to Fr Allan McDonald written between August 1901 and March 1902, without which evidence it would never have been known that Miss Freer had somehow come to grief and been discredited in the summer of 1901, relate to her career in psychical research, though they occur in letters of which the subject is Gaelic folklore.

Strange Things is now out of print. I am greatly indebted to my friend John Lorne Campbell for his willing agreement that my contribution to it, *The Strange Story of Ada Goodrich Freer*, which was complete in itself, be published as a separate book. This is being done concurrently with the re-issue of my *The Strange Case of Edmund Gurney*, first published in 1964 and made into a B.B.C. television play in 1967, and also now out of print. As Dr Campbell has pointed out, Miss Freer joined the S.P.R. in 1888, the year of Gurney's death, so that by coincidence the story of her extraordinary career extends the history of psychical research in Great Britain to the turn of the century. She quickly became a leading participant in the Society's activities, and a friend of some of the leading actors in the Gurney drama. These included persons of the stature of Professor Henry Sidgwick, and in particular F. W. H. Myers and G. A. Smith, the two extraordinary characters who in my opinion were responsible in their different ways for Gurney's tragedy. She also became associated with such fascinating figures of the period as John Patrick Crichton-Stuart (the third Marquess of Bute), William Hillier Onslow (the fourth Earl of Onslow), Lady Isabel Burton (the widow of Sir Richard Burton), William T. Stead, Sir William Huggins and Sir James Crichton-Browne.

One of the principal satisfactions to me of the long investigation described in this book was that much of it was based on previously unpublished material. Through the kindness of the present Marquess of Bute, for example, Dr Campbell and I were able to see copies of the whole of the third Marquess's large correspondence relating to psychical research. This material, which included over 95 letters from F. W. H. Myers alone, threw a flood of light on such previously unsolved cases as those of Ballechin House, Clandon Park and the Burton messages, in all of which Miss Freer was the central figure. I was thus enabled to write about them with the advantage of first-hand information before me, contained in letters written at the time. The Swanley mystery, which brought about Miss Freer's downfall and was unmentioned in the whole of the published literature of psychical research known to me, was a delight to investigate, since the original clues were limited to three references to the affair in unpublished correspondence at the turn of the century.

The invaluable assistance I have received in the solution of specific problems has been gratefully acknowledged in the text. I wish especially to thank, however, my friend John Lorne Campbell for the immense pleasure our collaboration afforded me, both in our large correspondence and our visits to each others' homes on the Isle of Canna and in Yorkshire, resulting in a happy companionship that has continued to the present day. It was my part in the writing of *Strange Things*, that first put my car on 'The Road to the Isles'.

It is a matter of deep satisfaction to me that another admired friend, Dr Eliot Slater, sometime Editor-in-Chief of *The British Journal of Psychiatry*, believes the personality of Ada Goodrich Freer to be of such interest that he has consented to write the Introduction to this book.

Selby, North Yorks.   T. H. H.

ILLUSTRATIONS

INTRODUCTION

by ELIOT SLATER, C.B.E., M.D., LL.D.
sometime Editor-in-Chief, *British Journal of Psychiatry*

It is sad that such a colourful personality as Ada Goodrich Freer could disappear so nearly irretrievably down the sink of time. This cannot have been her own wish. She must have had immortal longings, and even, with so many books and articles to her credit, a wish for fame. Yet she did everything she could to destroy the record of her life. She first appears fully grown, like Aphrodite from the waves, without a background or a past. She is thirty-one when she steps into the light of day; and even then she remains anonymous or a pseudonymous 'Miss X'. That she did not succeed in obliterating her origins and her true self we owe to the determined and successful researches of the indomitable Dr Trevor Hall. It is he who has dragged her back from oblivion to confront us with all her perversity, her charm and her deceits. In this short and rather speculative introduction to Dr Hall's far more solid work, I shall try to throw some light where Miss Freer threw the darkest of shadows.

When she was a child of only five and a half, in December 1862, Ada Freer suffered the terrible blow of losing her mother. A little more than three years later, in January 1866, her father also died. She was then left with her four brothers to the care of a widowed step-mother with a child of her own, and no family income to support them. Ada says she was brought up by 'an elderly relative with early Victorian standards'. Who was she? It was the reward of a remarkable voyage of discovery, with the aid of intuitive detective genius, that Dr Hall found out. Beyond reasonable doubt the elderly relative (very likely a great-aunt) is identified as a certain Miss Ann Adcock. This lady had a private boarding school for young ladies in Ilkley in Yorkshire, which is recorded in history from 1861 to 1875. The clues Dr Hall relied on were tenuous; and just how thorough his researches had to be are disclosed in an unobtrusive footnote. One might have known more about Miss Adcock's school, he remarks, but for the fact that it is not mentioned, either by advertisement or in any other way, in any issue of the *Ilkley Gazette* during those years. The results that Dr Hall achieves are not to be reached except at the expense of enormous labours, nearly always but not quite always spent in vain.

We see, then, this little girl of eight, orphaned of her father and mother, and now separated from her brothers and her home to be carried away to the north. We may feel sure that she was loved by her mother whom she lost when she was five; and it is probable that she was loved by her father who was taken from her three years later. One can suppose that as the only girl of the family, and a pretty little girl, she was loved and cosseted rather particularly. She also had a brother, just a year younger than her, on whom she in her turn would lavish love and attention. From this warm nest she was taken away. In the nature of things it must have been a desperately unhappy little girl who travelled to Ilkley with her elderly relative. To Ada she must have been an awesome figure, so old to a child's eyes, so much a headmistress, so unloved, so barely even known.

We must look at the situation also from Miss Adcock's point of view. She was a busy professional woman who had had her own school for the past five years. Somehow or other she had let family obligations and feelings of compassion run away with her. And now she was saddled with this child, her niece Mary's girl; and such a wretched unhappy child who, like Fanny Price in *Mansfield Park*, did not seem to realize and be grateful for all the immense benefits that were being conferred upon her.

One wonders how Ada settled down in Miss Adcock's school. In one sense her education was a great success. For when she re-emerged into the light of written record in 1888 she was a young woman of high intelligence, with many attainments (including some command of several languages), and the will and the capacity for very hard work. She had moreover the necessary social graces, poise and self-possession, agreeable manners and insinuating ways. We see her, seemingly much younger than her thirty-one years, with great physical attractions including beautiful grey eyes, and a captivating personality. She charmed and fascinated men of high social, academic and intellectual distinction. She used her abundant energy and her capacity for hard work for long periods at a stretch to produce papers on her chosen subjects which were highly regarded by the experts. The great Janet, the foremost psychologist of Europe before the days of Freud, was impressed by the exactitude and the importance of her observations on crystal-gazing.

The education she received in Miss Adcock's school was first-class, presumably imposed in a strictly disciplined way on a highly impressionable child. But, one would think, not a happy child. So much learning must have been at the expense of other joys and other freedoms. She said herself that she had supernormal experiences all through her childhood from the age of three. Such experiences, of any degree of vividness from day-dreaming to hallucination, depend on the capacity of the human mind for dissociation, a capacity which lessens with age and maturity. The fantasy life of the child may seem hardly less real than reality; and Ada Freer, who in her adult life was younger than her years in many ways, retained throughout her life the tendency to invent for herself a past more romantic and more glamorous than the truth. But a child that clings to fantasy is one for whom the real world is dreary or threatening; and the fact that Ada Freer depended so much upon fantasy suggests loneliness and unhappiness in her daily round.

In her time she must have been by far the cleverest girl in Miss Adcock's school. This could not have led to popularity with other girls, and as she was a diligent learner she would be despised as a swot. Being the relative of the proprietress and headmistress would also exclude her from friendships as a suspected favourite and potential or actual tale-bearer and sneak. It would be known that she came from a poor family and was getting her keep and her education free. The other girls no doubt came from prosperous homes. Class-conscious and money-conscious, they could not be expected to admit the charity girl to equality. One imagines that Ada would hardly have had a friend.

It would be no wonder if a friendless life at school encouraged those tendencies to secretiveness, subterfuge, fantasies, fabrications and a willingness to lie which she evinced in later life. On the credit side, she would have learned from her fellow pupils all the habitual ways of feeling, thinking and acting of county families. The vocabulary, the idiom and the pronunciation of the British upper middle class would come naturally. Later on she had no difficulty in acting the part of a girl with the right social background. This would not have helped her in her schooldays when everyone knew her origins. It might indeed have counted against her as much as all her other disadvantages. She could hardly have had a friend? Her record suggests that at school she never did have a friend, but remained as lonely when she left as when she arrived, since she carried no friendship with her into later years.

One of Ada Freer's most remarkable achievements was totally to prevent any knowledge by others of her birthplace, her family, her education and her life before she was introduced by Frederic Myers to the spiritualist scene. She covered over the facts by vague hints of socially elevated connections. Why? This course of deception involved her in considerable dangers. At any time a girl who had known her at school might meet her or see her and recognize her, and give the game away. There were dangers in every publication; and for years she remained a mere name and address on the books of the Society for

Psychical Research, while her contributions to the Society's Journal were safely covered by anonymity. Ada Freer certainly had the degree of respect for aristocratic connections which were typical of her time. But it seems unlikely that her past, by no means an uncreditable one, was so systematically concealed merely out of snobbery. The psychiatrist would suspect deeper motives. It looks as if she was trying to hide the past even from herself. One suspects she was trying to annihilate the girl she had been through childhood and adolescence, and if possible to forget long years of misery and guilt as if they had never been. After her period of anonymity she never could return to her born name. She was for every changing and embellishing it. She became successively Ada Goodrich-Freer, Adela Goodrich-Freer, Adela M. Goodrich-Freer, Adela Monica and finally A. Monica *née* Goodrich-Freer. It is at a cost that one denies one's country or one's kinship or one's childhood years, that one pulls oneself up by the roots, as it were, and amputates one great part of one's being. During the later years of her association with spiritualism and with Frederic Myers Ada Freer became a liar, a cheat and a thief of other men's work. She could hardly have sunk so far if she had not tried to destroy her own identity, and with it her self-image and her self-respect.

Miss Adcock's school apparently ceased to exist after 1875, when Ada was eighteen. We are left with no information at all about what happened to her during the next thirteen years. A reasonable guess would be that she continued to live with her Aunt Adcock as a companion until her death, and that she then left the north to come to London. There is a suggestion that for a few years she may have had a little money of her own, before it became absolutely necessary to earn her living. If so, it might have come as a bequest from her aunt. When she did seek a new life in the south the first of her contacts we know of (apart from her friend Constance Moore) was Frederic Myers. For him she would have many attractions. He was by temperament a Don Juan and Ada was an extremely fetching young woman. She had also another and more important claim to his attention in her capacity for dissociation, enabling her to see things in crystal balls and hear messages in sea-shells. And she had the intelligence and imagination to organize her experiences into plausible narrations. Myers may have trained her into capabilities which won her the high regard of spiritualists; or he may have merely encouraged her when she was trying these things out on her own. Certainly he was the influential member of the Society for Psychical Research who got her her entrée and started her on a way of life which provided her with a livelihood for a number of years. He may also have been her lover in the fullest or in some less than the full sense of the word.

Whatever his feelings for her, the relationship on her side was an intensely emotional one. This is shown by her fury at his entanglement with Iris Chaston and by the violence of her reaction when he finally threw her over. Myers was a wretched choice for a lover for any woman. He was a sensual but heartless egoist, a liar and a coward. Women and men, lovers and friends, he abandoned them all in any day of trouble. Frederic Myers is the only man we know of with whom Ada Freer may have had any kind of sex relationship until her marriage at the age of forty-eight. And yet she was an extremely attractive woman, and charmed and fascinated all the men with whom she came in contact. With women she was not such a success and in one or two provoked feelings of distrust and dislike.

All her life she looked about ten years younger than her real age. The photograph taken when she was thirty-seven shows a woman who looks much younger. She was a '*little* lady'; and with her round softly modelled face and tiny plump hands there is something childish, even babyish about her. The small stature goes well with her astonishing energy. There is no denying the magnitude of her labours, her persistence and her courage. The pyknic body-build, with round face and body and small hands and feet, is a natural biological foundation for an outgoing extraverted approach to life. In Ada's case it went also with winning ways and powers of sympathy that, we are told, seemed 'supernormal'.

Her childish looks may have been the reflection of a psychosexual immaturity. Her attractions for the male sex do not seem to have awakened in her any equal reciprocity. She was an unattached woman who could have had as many love affairs as she wished; but she seems to have felt no need of them. However she had a very long-lasting and intimate friendship with another woman, living for years with her and her family, or with her in an establishment of their own. Her relationship with Constance Moore lasted for twenty-one years from the time she was twenty-three until the critical years at the end of the century when things began to go wrong for her. The relationship must have been one of deep affection and, one would guess, most probably a love relationship with its sexual side. Despite the appeal she made to men, Ada Freer's sexual orientation was clearly not a fully normal heterosexual one. If we assume that it had an overtly homosexual aspect, much that is ambiguous and problematic about her would fall into place.

A sidelight of much interest is thrown by the letter passing between two ladies which is quoted on page 116. What is meant by Ada's invitation to one of them to go and 'stroke' her sometimes? It can hardly be doubted that a sexually toned contact is intended. 'Stroking' might mean no more than a caress, and culminate no further than in masturbation. But the context informs us that what is 'immense' enjoyment for the stroker might be hard to bear for the stroked; and Dr Dingwall has suggested that Miss Freer might have been seeking the pains and pleasures of flagellation. If so, it would be entirely in character. Those to whom normal love relationships do not come easily, commonly find an outlet in substitute sexuality.

During the latter half of the nineteenth century in Britain the corporal punishment of children was very common, more so in schools than at home, and above all in boarding schools. The site of chastisement was either the hand or the buttocks, perhaps the former more for girls and the latter for boys, but in the main indifferently for either sex. The cutaneous nerve supply of the buttocks is part of that of a wider region including the genitals; and stimulation in that area, even if sharp and painful, could irradiate the wider network and give rise to strongly pleasurable sexual sensations. The habituation of children and young persons to such conditioning, in the unfortunates who were susceptible, could sometimes lead to a sexual perversion—so commonly in fact that in other countries the many forms of flagellation came to be known as the English vice. If Ada Freer at the age of forty-three was asking a friend to give her sexual relief in this way (at about the time when she was parting from Constance Moore), it suggests that such experiences had been part of her life for many years. One would think that the tendency had in fact been instilled during early years of sexual maturation at Miss Adcock's boarding school for young ladies. Ada Freer's letters show her to have been rather prim, very aware of Mrs Grundy and the *convenances*. Such secret sexual urges as we are led to suspect would have been a cause of ever-recurring guilt, an obstacle between her and any normal love relationship with a man, something more easily and less shamefully satisfied in a lesbian than a heterosexual relationship. Whatever the enjoyment of her friend, it seems unlikely that what Ada Freer was asking for was a merely erotic experience. 'She couldn't stand it, if it didn't do her some good' we read; and this suggests a severity in handling which reminds one of the rigours demanded by such eminent masochists as Algernon Charles Swinburne and T. E. Lawrence. This unhappy woman must have felt a strong need for self-punishment. She may have hoped that, as with the saints, it would be good for the soul; and her soul was in need of healing.

It was indeed about this time, starting towards the end of 1900 and extending through till at least August of the next year that Ada Freer had her one and only nervous illness. It took, typically, the form of a depression. The psychological causes, if they extended, are not obvious. It was three years since her quarrel with Myers; and she had survived the discredit of the Ballechin fiasco without weakening. She had lost the support of a generous friend, it is true, by the death of Lord Bute in October 1900. In a person of Ada Freer's pyknic build and syntonic personality, however, one is inclined to think that biological rather than psychological factors would have been the main cause. And forty-three is about the age of the change of life. In due course she found her way through the depression, and as far as we know never suffered a relapse.

It was perhaps because Miss Freer was still depressed, still felt tired, and was lacking in resource and inventiveness, in that fateful year of 1901, that she chanced her hand with a technique which was beyond her skill. Perhaps, also, she had lost heart for trickery and she could not go through with it with confidence and conviction. Perhaps, even, so strange is the human heart, there was an unconscious wish to be caught out, to accept her punishment, and to be quit of the career of a professional spiritualist for ever. It was inspired work on the part of Dr Hall to trace the tenuous connections which link a reference in a letter, a footnote in a heavy tome, the destruction of certain files of the S.P.R. and the identification of one of its members as a clergyman in Swanley, and so to offer us a satisfying explanation of the catastrophe which at last exposed Ada Freer as a cheat. It led to her abandoning all her past labours, her interests, her friendships and her circle of acquaintances, to leave Britain for ever.

One can hope that after these storms she enjoyed some sunshine in her later years. We have no reason for thinking that her husband did not truly love her or that the marriage was not a happy one. To the end she persuaded her husband, and may have half-believed herself, that she was many years younger than her true age, perhaps even that those years which she preferred to forget had in some sense never really existed. In these latter years she was as energetic as ever, travelled much and wrote a number of books. She died at the age of seventy-three of heart failure following on hypertensive heart disease. This is a stress disease, and can be related to the anxieties and tensions, the hard work, the frustrations, the sadness and the disappointments of her life. But for them, with her gift for enduring youth, she should have been able to live on into her eighties or even nineties, failing some killing disease like cancer. Her last noteworthy act was to arrange that an important document, annotated by her, actually reached a library where it would be available in perpetuity. A sign of grace and recognition of responsibility, one may think.

It is difficult to know how much of the truth there was in her. Early on, as a child and young woman, she must have been convinced of the 'reality' of some of her supernormal experiences. The months of work she put in at the library of the British Museum in 1887 to write her long and scholarly work on the history of crystal-gazing must have been sustained by a firm belief in the authenticity of the experiences gained in this way by herself and by countless others before her. It was Frederic Myers who put the crystal into her hands, and it may be that he was her evil genius throughout. One is tempted to believe that bit by bit she came to discard her faith in this and perhaps in all other avenues to occult knowledge. For a time she was willing cynically to exploit the self-deceptions of others. The attempted fraud on Lady Burton can hardly have been other than clear-sightedly wicked. It looks as if sincerity came to her in the end and she was left disgusted by herself. Her attack on mediums cost her all her friends with the exception of Lord Bute's family. It was made regardlessly of her interests (in a prudential sense), and can only have been carried out at the urge of deep and powerful emotions. It coincided with the giving away of her psychic library. These acts constitute a denial of the whole meaning of her life until that time. In effect they were a recantation and a spectacular act of self-punishment. Such behaviour can hardly be understood except as the manifest sign of a change of heart.

This introduction to Dr Hall's book has been, of course, a piece of self-indulgence on the part of the writer, intrigued beyond measure by the enigma of a personality. Poor justice has been done to the absorbing interest of Dr Hall's complex and beautiful detective story, and none to the picture he gives us of a world so close to us in historical time, so distant in standards and beliefs and all the complexities that go to make a society. Ada Freer is only one, if the strangest, of the many odd and quirky personalities who lived in that world. In Dr Hall's story, as it cannot be in a work of fiction, not one but all of them move and breathe and are individuals in their own right. Let the reader then turn to the pages that follow. He may, if he wishes, check the psychiatrist's interpretations against conclusions of his own, or forget them entirely.

E. S.

1

THE MYSTERY OF 'MISS X'

IN DECEMBER 1964 Dr John Lorne Campbell sent me a copy of his booklet, *The Late Fr Allan McDonald, Miss Goodrich Freer and Hebridean Folklore*.[1] This essay showed that a substantial part of the literary remains of Fr Allan McDonald of Eriskay, which Dr Campbell was preparing for publication, had been unscrupulously used by the late Miss Freer over her own name in the furtherance of her literary career as a self-styled authority on Scottish Gaelic folklore.

Dr Campbell asked whether I had any information in my library regarding Miss Freer. His enquiry had been prompted by the reading of my book on the mysterious circumstances surrounding the death in 1888 of Edmund Gurney,[2] the Hon. Secretary of the Society for Psychical Research, an organization of which Miss Freer had been a prominent member from the year of Gurney's death to the turn of the century. I was asked if I knew anything of Miss Freer's personal life and antecedents, and of the activities in psychical research with which she had been preoccupied before embarking upon her career as a folklorist. In particular, Dr Campbell enquired whether I could throw any light upon an incident which had taken place in the village of Swanley, Kent, in which Miss Freer had been involved, evidently not to her credit, and to which Dr Campbell had discovered an unpublished reference in Fr Allan's papers. This occurrence, whatever it was, had soon been followed by Miss Freer's relinquishment of her membership of the S.P.R., and her departure from England to Jerusalem at the end of 1901.[3]

At the time I received Dr Campbell's letter my knowledge of

---

[1] Reprinted from *Scottish Studies*, 1958, vol. II, pp. 175–88.

[2] *The Strange Case of Edmund Gurney*, London, 1964.

[3] It is true that Miss Freer's last entry in the membership lists of the S.P.R. was in January 1903, but she had undoubtedly left England before then. This is clear from an unpublished letter from Miss Ruth Landon to Fr Allan of 15th December 1901, in which she referred to the fact that Miss Freer was already on her way to Port Said. The preface to Miss Freer's book, *Outer Isles*, was written in Jerusalem in May 1902.

Miss Freer was little more than superficial. I was aware that she had been an early and highly regarded member of the S.P.R., had made substantial contributions to the Society's *Proceedings*, and had written two books on psychical research, *The Alleged Haunting of B[allechin] House* (with Lord Bute, a Vice-President of the S.P.R.) and *Essays in Psychical Research*, both published in 1899.[1] I knew that Miss Freer had been the assistant editor of the spiritualist periodical *Borderland*. Her photograph had shown her to be an attractive woman, and I had been told that in some circles an affair between Miss Freer and F. W. H. Myers, one of the founders of the S.P.R., had been suspected.

An interesting discovery involving Miss Freer had been made during my investigation of the life and death of Edmund Gurney. Just as Eleanor and Arthur Sidgwick, the biographers of Henry Sidgwick, the first President of the S.P.R., in *Henry Sidgwick, A Memoir* (London, 1906), had suppressed that part of his 'Journal' in which Sidgwick had revealed his doubts about the supposed accidental circumstances of Gurney's death, so had they also thought it expedient to conceal from the reader Sidgwick's references to certain incidents connecting Miss Freer and F. W. H. Myers.[2] This was about the limit of my original knowledge of the lady in whom Dr Campbell was interested, except that I think I recalled at the time, from a note in the late Harry Price's *Short-Title Catalogue of Works on Psychical Research, etc.* (London, 1929), that at a later period of her life Miss Freer had married Dr Hans H. Spoer. Biographical enquiry is, however, very congenial to me, and I welcomed the opportunity of offering such assistance as I could in solving the problems which Dr Campbell had outlined in his letter.

A considerable correspondence soon developed between Dr Campbell and myself, which ultimately led to the kind suggestion that we should collaborate in the preparation of this book. The matter was of great interest to me for more than one reason. First, it has been invariably urged by believers in psychical phenomena that educated, intellectually gifted, and socially accomplished persons like Miss Freer, who claim so-called supernormal powers, can never in the nature of things be fraudulent, because of the lack of any obvious motive. The consistent attitude of researchers in this field, since the formation of the S.P.R. in 1882 to the present day, is that

[1] A second and revised edition of *The Alleged Haunting of B—— House* was published in 1900.

[2] The extracts from the MS. of Henry Sidgwick's 'Journal', now in the Library of Trinity College, Cambridge, were very kindly made for me by Dr A. R. G. Owen. They are referred to in more detail later.

stories by such individuals of their experiences, however improbable and uncorroborated, must be accepted without question.[1] The case of Miss Freer, whose accounts of her crystal visions, shell-hearing, and telepathic abilities were accepted with implicit belief and enthusiastic praise by leaders of the S.P.R. of the stature of Professor Henry Sidgwick and F. W. H. Myers, seems to be an appropriate subject for enquiry in this connexion. Secondly, a study of the career of this lady, and her relationships with those eminent Victorians who were interested in occult matters, adds significantly to our knowledge of the melancholy history of psychical research in England during the period from the climacteric of the death of Edmund Gurney to the end of the nineteenth century.

The circumstances of the birth and early life of Ada Goodrich Freer are of importance to our understanding of the motives and psychology of this extraordinary woman. She enjoyed the advantage, apparently throughout her adult life, of appearing to be at least ten years younger than her actual age, with personal attractions which seem to have been almost hypnotic in their effect, and which she used irresistibly and ruthlessly upon those whom she thought could be of use to her.[2] These qualities were combined with remarkable energy and a formidable intelligence. There is a good deal of evidence to suggest, however, that she suffered from *folie de grandeur*. As an example, she quarrelled bitterly with F. W. H. Myers in 1897, and he became seriously ill early in 1898. Miss Freer wrote to Lord Bute on 28th March 1898, pointing out that Myers had never been ill in his life before and that 'those who hate or oppose me always come to grief'. She claimed that she could quote a score of other cases in which this had happened, and that she had in consequence and in charity to exercise restraint in forming dislikes for people.[3] She was indeed a strange person, and it is therefore unfortunate that she was consistently both deceitful and secretive about her antecedents and upbringing, thereby making this part of the enquiry both protracted and difficult, and in some respects still incomplete.

[1] For an authoritative comment on what Dr E. J. Dingwall has called 'this naïve belief', the reader is referred to his 'British Investigation of Spontaneous Cases', *International Journal of Parapsychology*, 1961, vol. II, pp. 89–97. It is discussed on pp. 63 ff. of my *The Strange Case of Edmund Gurney*.

[2] In an unpublished letter of 13th July 1894 the Rev. Peter Dewar, in the first flush of his enthusiasm for Miss Freer, wrote to Lord Bute that her powers of sympathy seemed to him to be supernormal, and that she could get into living, sympathetic touch with people as no others could do. Fr Allan McDonald wrote of Miss Freer in his diary on 9th September 1897, 'My acquaintance with her has been an education of mind and soul, and has thrown sunshine over the last two years of my life.'

[3] An unpublished letter.

When Miss Freer (then Mrs H. H. Spoer) entered St Luke's Hospital, New York, on 20th December 1930 suffering from 'hypertensive heart disease', to die there on 24th February 1931, her age was recorded as fifty-six. This information, suggesting that she was born in 1874, was presumably given either by Miss Freer herself or her husband. As Dr Spoer was sixteen years younger than his wife, he himself may have been misinformed regarding her age. It is admittedly hard to credit that Dr Spoer could really have believed that his wife was fifty-six when she was actually seventy-three, but the fact that the former incorrect age is also recorded at Cedar Lawn Cemetery, Patterson, New Jersey, where Miss Freer is buried, would suggest that this was so. On the other hand, it seems probable, to say the least of it, that Dr Spoer knew that the statement on his wife's death certificate that she had lived in the United States for twenty-six years was untrue to the extent of at least fourteen years, as is demonstrated by her entries in *Who's Who*.[1]

Official and semi-official sources offer little information about Miss Freer's personal life. In none of her twenty-five entries in *Who's Who* did she disclose anything whatsoever of her date or place of birth, her parentage or place of education. The single piece of biographical information offered is that she married Dr Spoer in 1905. The same withholding of any clue as to whom she was or where she came from is repeated in her many books, and in the whole of her voluminous writings in *Folklore*, *The Occult Review*, *Borderland*, *The Nineteenth Century*, the *Proceedings* and the *Journal* of the Society for Psychical Research, and the other periodicals to which she contributed. Indeed, during the initial ten years of her published work on psychical research and kindred subjects from 1889 she preferred at first to remain completely anonymous, later using the pseudonym 'Miss X'.

Previously unpublished correspondence, now available to Dr Campbell and myself, is no more helpful in this regard than the printed sources. According to the late Lady Margaret MacRae (formerly Lady Margaret Crichton-Stuart), the daughter of Miss Freer's patron Lord Bute, the family was informed by Miss Freer that she was a relative of Sir Bartle Freer [*sic*].[2] On the other hand,

---

[1] See p. 126.
[2] Sir Henry Bartle Edward Frere (1815–84), K.C.B., G.C.S.I., D.C.L. (Oxon.), LL.D. (Cantab.), F.R.S., statesman and Governor of Bombay, was commonly called Sir Bartle Frere. He ranks twenty columns in the *Dictionary of National Biography*. His statue on the Thames Embankment was unveiled by the Prince of Wales in 1888. On 10th October 1844 he married Miss Catherine Arthur, the daughter of Sir George Arthur of Bombay. Quite apart

4

Miss Freer (who by that time was calling herself Goodrich-Freer) told Lord Bute in her letter of 9th December 1895 that 'my father and all my deceased family were Goodrich'. It seems impossible to reconcile this statement with the fact that investigation has shown that her father was George Freer and that her mother's maiden name was Adcock. Miss Freer's second forename derived from her paternal grandmother, who before her marriage to William Freer was Ann Goodrich, the daughter of a wheelwright in Rutland.

These facts regarding Miss Freer's parentage also throw the gravest doubt upon her story to Lord and Lady Bute in 1898 that Dr John Bacchus Dykes (1823–76), the distinguished musician and divine, was her uncle.[1] Before her marriage to Dr Dykes, his wife was Miss Susan Kingston, the daughter of George Kingston of Malton. Dr Dykes's mother's maiden name was Elizabeth Huntington, the daughter of a Hull surgeon. The biography of Dr Dykes contains no reference whatever to any Freer, Adcock, or Goodrich.[2] What it does reveal is that Fr Thomas Dykes, who embraced the Roman Catholic faith in 1851 and became a Jesuit priest, was the elder brother of Dr J. B. Dykes, who Miss Freer claimed as her uncle. Yet, in a letter to Lord Bute of 5th March 1897 she stated that Fr Thomas Dykes was her cousin.

The suspicion that these claims by Miss Freer to intimate connexions with distinguished families may have been manufactured to impress Lord Bute and others is not diminished by another very odd story told by her. Paulet is, of course, the family name of the Marquess of Winchester. At the end of 1895 Miss Freer wrote to Lord Bute to say that she had received a paranormal message at the moment of his death from 'my dear old friend Stuart Paulet, who was brought up with me and has been far more of a brother to me than my own ever were'.[3] She did not learn of his death by normal means, she added, until four days after her experience. She wrote that five years previously, in 1890, she and Paulet had quarrelled and as a result he had left England, a somewhat dramatic departure for

---

[1] This story was vaguely supported by a claim by Miss Freer in her essay, 'The Mystic Musician', that in earlier years she had lived in the household of a distinguished musician (*Borderland*, 1894–5, vol. II, p. 422).

[2] J. T. Fowler, *Life and Letters of John Bacchus Dykes, M.A., Mus.Doc.*, London, 1897.

[3] Neither Burke, Debrett, nor Walford make mention of any Stuart Paulet. The Lists of Members of Oxford and Cambridge Universities of the period also fail to record anyone of this name. No obituary has been traced.

---

from the difference in the names, I am not aware of a shred of evidence to connect him with Miss Freer.

which his parents had blamed Miss Freer. Paulet was, said Miss Freer, 'impulsive and romantic'. She said that in 1887 she and Paulet had been through a crisis in their religious opinions, 'as most thoughtful young people do'. Miss Freer was thirty in 1887.

A useful background to the truth or otherwise of these assertions by Miss Freer about herself to Lord Bute and his family was her claim to have been one of the first women to become a Fellow of the Royal Society. This was recorded by Lord Colum Crichton-Stuart, Lord Bute's son, in a letter to the late Miss S. R. Dowling in terms that make it plain that Miss Freer had convinced the Bute family that she did enjoy this distinction. The facts in regard to the election of women to Fellowship of the Royal Society are of interest in this connexion, and I am indebted to the Society and its Librarian for kindly supplying them.

In January 1902 a certificate of candidature in favour of Mrs H. Ayrton was received and declined in the face of legal advice that the Society could not elect women under its Charters and Statutes. This first became possible under the Sex Disqualification (Removal) Act 1919, but it was not until 1944 that the Statutes of the Royal Society were actually amended to enable women to be elected. Miss Freer was never an F.R.S., and had indeed been dead thirteen years before she could have become one. The first two ladies to be appointed Fellows were Dr Kathleen Lonsdale (now Dame Kathleen Lonsdale) and the late Dr Marjory Stephenson. Both were elected in 1945.

Confidence in Miss Freer's adherence to the truth in her correspondence with her patron Lord Bute is not increased by her assertion in her letter of 23rd March 1896 that her brother was at Oxford with Lord Onslow. The circumstances of the upbringing of Miss Freer and her brothers, to be discussed later in this chapter, were not such as would make it seem probable that any of them were at Oxford. However that may be, the facts are that those of Miss Freer's brothers who did not die in infancy, Benjamin, George, Arthur, and Ernest, were born respectively in 1849, 1851, 1854, and 1858. William Hillier Onslow (1853–1911), the fourth Earl, entered Exeter College, Oxford, on 15th April 1871 and left in 1872 after rather more than a year without sitting for any of the university examinations.[1] The *Oxford University Calendar* of 1872, which shows Lord Onslow as a commoner of Exeter, also lists a Benjamin

---

[1] J. Foster, *Alumni Oxonienses*, Oxford, 1888, vol. III, p. 1043, and *Dictionary of National Biography*.

John Michael Freer as an undergraduate and bible clerk of Oriel. If casual enquiry was limited to this single source, therefore, it might seem possible that Miss Freer's story could have been true, although it is fair to point out that her eldest brother, born in Uppingham, Rutland, on 16th June 1849, was simply 'Benjamin Freer', according to his birth certificate.

On the assumption that Miss Freer took the risk of fabricating her statement to Lord Bute after an examination of the *Oxford University Calendar* for the two years of Lord Onslow's short period at the university (and if she did not, then the coincidence that a Benjamin Freer was actually at Oxford at the relevant time is an extraordinary one), it is a pity that she did not take the additional precaution of also consulting Foster's *Alumni Oxonienses*. This work of reference would have told her that additional information was in print, which could have been seen by Lord Bute, which demolished her story completely. Benjamin John Michael Freer was not Miss Freer's brother but the second son of Thomas Freer of Kirk Braddan in the Isle of Man.[1] The extraordinary fact is that he entered Oriel College in 1855 at the age of eighteen, and was still an undergraduate in 1872 at the age of thirty-five.

There remains one puzzling aspect of what appears to have been a singularly reckless piece of deception on the part of Miss Freer. It will be recalled that in an earlier letter to Lord Bute of 9th December 1895 she had falsely claimed that her father's name was really Goodrich. Of the eleven members of the university of this name one only, Laurence Charles Goodrich, was at Oxford, and indeed at Exeter College, at the same time as Lord Onslow. Miss Freer had no brother named Laurence, of course. Laurence Goodrich was the fifth son of James Pitt Goodrich, gentleman, of Maisemore, Gloucestershire, and entered Exeter College on 21st January 1871.[2] He was clearly not Miss Freer's brother, and it seems difficult to believe, moreover, that the Maisemore family had any close connexion with Miss Freer's paternal grandmother, Ann Goodrich, the daughter of a wheelwright in Rutland. However this may be, the fact that there was a Goodrich of good family at Exeter College with Lord Onslow at the relevant time makes one wonder whether Miss Freer intended Lord Bute to believe that her brother at Oxford was Laurence Goodrich or Benjamin Freer. Her previous story that her father's name was Goodrich supported one claimant, while the fact that she

---

[1] *Alumni Oxonienses*, vol. II, p. 494. The Treasurer of Oriel College has very kindly confirmed the facts regarding B. J. M. Freer.

[2] *Alumni Oxonienses*, vol. III, p. 538.

had a brother named Benjamin supported the other. We can take the matter no further.[1]

Such information as has been published about the date of Miss Freer's birth has been both varied and incorrect. The Folklore Society, which she joined in 1893, believed that she was born in 1870,[2] presumably from particulars supplied by her when she applied for membership. Her card in the Catalogue of the Library of Congress, on the other hand, records her year of birth as 1865,[3] as do her entries in the *Literary Year-Book and Bookman's Directory*. As has been said, the particulars supplied to St Luke's Hospital, New York, and repeated in Miss Freer's death certificate, indicate her year of birth as 1874. Ada Goodrich Freer was, in fact, born on 15th May 1857.[4]

The earliest book of reference that I have been able to discover containing her name is the List of Members of the Society for Psychical Research. She joined this organization on 28th January 1888 as an Associate, first describing herself simply as 'Miss Freer'.[5] When she was awarded the distinction of Honorary Associateship and relieved of her subscription in 1893, in recognition of what was regarded as her outstanding work for the Society, this was amended to 'Miss A. Goodrich Freer'. By August of the same year, however, she began to hyphenate her name as 'Goodrich-Freer' in the

[1] The incident that caused Miss Freer to assert that her family name was really Goodrich was a séance held in London at which the medium was Mrs Everitt, whose career had begun as early as 1855. Miss Freer wrote scornfully to Lord Bute about this séance, referring to the medium's 'cockney twang' and to the 'silly drivel' of her communications. 'The grand test offered, was that though I was introduced as Miss X, the spirits called me "Freer", and brought me messages of the "Be good" type from deceased Freers, the fact being that my Father and all my deceased family were Goodrich!' The cynical reader may well suspect that Mrs Everitt may have revealed some embarrassing truth about Miss Freer's origin at this séance, which might well have surprised Lord Bute, had it reached his ears without previous contradiction.

[2] This date is given in her obituary, published by the Society in its official journal, *Folklore*, 1931, vol. XLI, pp. 299–301. The obituary was written by the Editor at the time, A. R. Wright, F.S.A., who remarked that it was greatly to be desired that a biography should be written of a life so noteworthy. He can scarcely have realized how difficult such a task might be.

[3] This date is given in the printed catalogue as '1865–'.

[4] This name is recorded on her birth certificate, where her parents are shown as George and Mary Freer. On her New York death certificate, however, her father's name is enlarged to George Goodrich Freer. The fact that she was born in Uppingham, Rutland, was not revealed.

[5] *Journal*, S.P.R., February 1888, p. 221. Her promotion was rapid. In the first List of Members published after her election, made as at May 1889, in *Proceedings*, 1888–9, vol. V, she was already shown as a full member.

membership list. In 1907, when her name first appeared in *Who's Who*, she added an extra initial and was there shown as 'A. M. Goodrich-Freer', this being repeated in all her subsequent entries, which continued until 1931, the year of her death. In the British Museum Catalogue her name is given as 'Ada M. Goodrich Freer'.[1] She started to call herself 'Adela Goodrich-Freer' in the *Literary Year-Book and Bookman's Directory* in 1907, having described herself as 'Ada Goodrich-Freer' in the issues up to 1906. In the Library of Congress Catalog she is described as 'Adela M. Goodrich-Freer'.

On her death certificate her name is recorded as 'Adela Monica Spoer', while in her obituary in *Folklore* she is referred to as '[Mrs] Adela Monica Goodrich-Freer Spoer (1870–1931)'. It seems probable that in her later years she was known by her invented name of Monica, for her tombstone is inscribed 'A. Monica, née Goodrich-Freer, wife of H. Henry Spoer'.[2]

During the investigation of Miss Freer's life it has become apparent that little reliance can be placed upon her statements in regard to her antecedents and upbringing (with the names of persons and places consistently omitted or disguised under mere initials) implying that she came from a distinguished and well-to-do family in the North of England and was of Scottish descent. I myself doubt the truth of either of these suggestions. So far as Ada Freer's alleged Scottish forebears are concerned, it may be pointed out that her father, grandfather, and great-grandfather were all residents of the town of Uppingham, in Rutland, in the English Midlands. She herself was born there, a fact which she concealed throughout the whole of her adult life. Although, according to the present rector, none of the family survive there today, the Freers were established in Uppingham from the middle of the eighteenth century at the latest. We find from the church register, for example, that on 12th December 1751 Henry Exton married Susanna Freer, followed by numerous and regular entries of baptisms, marriages, and burials of Freers in Uppingham during the intervening years to 1812, when William Freer, Ada's grandfather and the son of John Freer, a carpenter, married Ann Goodrich. The reader may think that if the Scottish ancestors existed, they were too remote adequately to justify, for example, Miss Freer's statement to the Rev.

---

[1] *British Museum General Catalogue of Printed Books*, vol. 79, London, 1961.
[2] It is of interest that Fr Allan McDonald wrote in his diary on 4th May 1898 'St Monica's [day]. Said Mass for Miss Freer.' This suggests that she had an interest in St Monica for a number of years before adopting the name.

Peter Dewar, in a letter dated 25th May 1894 on the subject of her extreme suitability for the Scottish Second Sight Enquiry, that she was 'of Scotch blood (Aberdeen), and [I] belong to a family which has possessed the gift of second sight for many generations', or her claim in her lecture to the Gaelic Society of Inverness in April 1896 that she spoke as a Highlander to Highlanders,[1] or her published remark in the same year that she proudly claimed the Scots as her fellow-countrymen.[2] It may be pointed out in this connexion that these observations in regard to her alleged Scottish descent were all made during the period when she was seeking or enjoying the patronage of the wealthy Lord Bute,[3] a convinced Scottish nationalist and an advocate of Scottish home rule, who had devoted much time to a long and intensive study of Scottish history and institutions.

The well-to-do 'county' family background claimed by Miss Freer also seems to fall to pieces when examined. The index to the *Victoria History of the County of Rutland* (London, 1936), which contains every family of any importance in England's smallest county, makes no mention of the names of either Freer or Goodrich. I see no reason for stretching the imagination to suppose that either Dr Frier, a master at Oakham School in 1649, or the Rev. Thomas Frere (d. 1667), Rector of Whitwell, had any direct connexion with the Freers of Uppingham, a family of tradesmen. Neither of the two issues of *The Visitation of the County of Rutland*, published in London by the Harleian Society in 1870 and 1922, contains the name Freer, either in their indexes or in the quite exhaustive lists of families whose pedigrees are there traced. It would seem, moreover, that as late as the end of the eighteenth century some of the Uppingham Freers were without education. When George Chilton, a soldier of the Durham Regiment of Militia, married Sarah Freer of Uppingham on 9th December 1799 both bride and bridegroom signed the church register with an 'X'.

One cannot avoid, indeed, the melancholy conclusion that many of Miss Freer's references to herself were calculated to mislead her readers. She wrote, for example:

---

[1] She did not say that she was born in Scotland, and indeed conceded that she was 'born south of the Tweed', less fortunately than her forebears (*Transactions of the Gaelic Society of Inverness*, vol. XXI, p. 106).

[2] *Borderland*, 1896, vol. III, p. 61.

[3] In a letter to her mother, the Marchioness of Bute, of 1st June 1901, Lady Margaret MacRae wrote, 'How cross she [Miss Freer] would be if she thought you didn't think her Scotch. She isn't a bit, but always says she is, and her Scottish stories and accent would make a cow laugh.'

*I belong to no effete race, but to a family which for physique and
longevity might challenge any in the annals of Mr Francis Galton;—a
family which has never lived in cities, and which, for many generations,
has expended its energies and ambitions on horses and hounds.*[1]

So far as longevity is concerned, it is pertinent to point out that
Miss Freer's father and mother died at the ages of forty-six and
forty-five respectively, while her grandmother only lived to be
thirty-eight. Her aunt died at twenty-seven. Her sister Ann and two
of her brothers died in infancy. On the subject of the absorption of
'many generations' of her forebears in horses and hounds, it is
relevant to mention that Miss Freer's grandfather was a wheelwright, and her great-grandfather a carpenter. It is true that Miss
Freer's father was a veterinary surgeon,[2] but whether that was the
impression Miss Freer intended to convey by her reference to horses
and hounds is, I fancy, open to question. It seems to me more likely
to be part of the pattern of the grooms and gardeners who told her
ghost stories as a child, the dear old family servants she had known
all her life and the other ingredients of the vague, affluent, country-
house background she created for her autobiographical asides.

It is unfortunate and somewhat remarkable that, apart from her
many letters to Lord Bute, now available for the first time, virtually
all original papers and correspondence relating to Miss Freer seem
to have disappeared. From 1893 to 1897 Miss Freer was employed
by W. T. Stead as his assistant editor of the occult magazine *Borderland*, but the correspondence between Stead and Miss Freer, and
indeed all the papers connected with *Borderland*, seem to have
vanished completely, according to Stead's biographer, Professor
J. O. Baylen, of the University of Georgia.[3] The Folklore Society,
of which she was a member for nearly thirty-eight years, knows

---

[1] *Proceedings*, S.P.R., 1892, vol. VIII, p. 484. Miss Freer was probably referring to Sir Francis Galton's *Human Faculty* (London, 1883), and to *Natural
Inheritance* (London, 1889) by the same author.

[2] In her letter of 24th January 1896 to Lord Bute, Miss Freer wrote that her
father had studied medicine before his elder brother died, 'but never took his
degree or practised', thus implying that he was a person of leisure and inherited
wealth.

[3] Professor Baylen has written to Dr Campbell to say that it almost looks as if
what material there may have been among the Stead papers relating to Miss
Freer has been removed by someone at some time. If this is so, then such
removal must have taken place after the publication of Frederic Whyte's *The Life
of W. T. Stead*, 2 vols., London, 1925, for in this book there are several references
to correspondence between Stead and Miss Freer. It is, incidentally, curious
that in another life of Stead, published in 1913, *My Father*, written by Stead's
daughter, Miss Estelle W. Stead, there is no mention of Miss Freer at all,
although the publication of *Borderland* is discussed at some length.

virtually nothing about her which is not available in *Who's Who*. Her obituary in *Folklore* gives no details of her early life, and contains many errors of fact in addition to the mistake of thirteen years in her date of birth. Not long before his death in 1951 Dr H. H. Spoer wrote to Dr Campbell to say that all his wife's papers had been lost or destroyed in the course of their travels in the Near East.

She was a leading member of the Society for Psychical Research from 1888 until 1902, and her photograph is included in the Society's album, 'English Portraits', of the distinguished members and associates of early years. She claimed to be an officer of the Society[1] and a member of several of its Committees.[2] She presented several long papers to the Society on crystal-gazing, telepathic experiences, clairvoyance, and similar subjects, under the chairmanship of various presidents, including Henry Sidgwick and William Crookes. She had been intimately acquainted with F. W. H. Myers, one of the founders of the Society, and had known well other presidents such as Mrs Henry Sidgwick and Andrew Lang. Among many other activities and writings, she was the Council's representative for the three investigations into second sight in the Highlands and the Islands of Scotland in 1894, 1895, and 1896, paid for by Lord Bute, a Vice-President of the S.P.R. She was the medium through whom the famous messages, allegedly from the spirit of Sir Richard Burton, were received in 1895, and about which she lectured to the Society. She was mainly responsible for the enquiry into the alleged haunting of Ballechin House, in Perthshire, in 1897. Yet all the files dealing with these and other matters connected with Miss Freer have disappeared. The present officers of the Society say that they do not now possess any documents relating to her apart from the single photograph mentioned. The fact that no obituary was published in either the *Journal* or the *Proceedings* of the Society is presumably explained by the fact that although to the end of her life Miss Freer claimed to be a member in her entries in *Who's Who*, she had in reality ceased to have any connexion with the S.P.R. for nearly thirty years at the time of her death.

[1] A. Goodrich-Freer and John, Marquess of Bute, *The Alleged Haunting of B—— House*, new and revised edition, London, 1900, p. xiii.

[2] A. Goodrich-Freer, *Essays in Psychical Research*, London, 1899, p. 16.

2

MISS FREER'S ANTECEDENTS

THE MORE immediate history of Miss Freer's forebears began on 13th July 1812 in Uppingham. On that day William Freer, a wheelwright and the son of an Uppingham carpenter named John Freer, married Ann, daughter of Thomas and Elizabeth Goodrich. Ann died in Uppingham on 14th January 1828 aged thirty-eight, after having given birth to many children. After Ann's death William married again, and his second wife was buried in the same grave in Uppingham churchyard as Ann. On 25th December 1852 William married yet again. His third wife was another Ann, daughter of an Uppingham labourer, John Kirby. William did not long survive this marriage and died on 7th August 1853.

While it is true that the Victorians produced larger families than we do today, the alacrity with which both Miss Freer's grandfather and father entered into further unions so soon after bereavements suggests that one attribute of the family was unusual sexual vigour, which may offer some explanation of Miss Freer's extraordinary energy. In her letter to the Rev. Peter Dewar in 1894, published for the first time elsewhere in this book,[1] she said that she delighted in an outdoor life and could ride, swim, and sail a boat, which may well be true, although her unfortunate lack of adherence to the truth about herself in her writings could cause the sceptic to doubt her statement that she rose early each day and walked six to twelve miles in all weathers[2] as a relief from her intellectual preoccupations. There can be no doubt at all, however, on the evidence of her published work and correspondence, about the immensity of her labours, the extreme diligence and ability with which she studied the unusual subjects to which she devoted most of her life, and the

[1] See p. 10.

[2] *Proceedings*, S.P.R., 1895, vol. VIII, p. 484. On 25th May of the previous year she told the Rev. Peter Dewar, in the same letter referred to above, that her walking averaged sixteen miles a day! And if this amount of physical exercise was not enough, Miss Freer claimed in an article extolling the virtues of horticulture as an appropriate activity for educated persons, published in *The Nineteenth Century*, November 1899, that she had been an enthusiastic practical gardener from her earliest childhood.

persistence with which she pursued her social and literary ambitions.

George Freer was born in 1820 and was one of William Freer's children by his first wife Ann Goodrich. On 16th September 1847 he married Mary, the daughter of Josiah Adcock, also of Uppingham, by whom he had eight children, whose birth certificates are before me as I write. They were: Benjamin, b. 1849; Ann, b. 1850, who died in the same year; George, b. 1851; Arthur, b. 1854; Ada Goodrich, b. 1857; Ernest, b. 1858; an unnamed twin with Ernest, who lived only one hour; and William Howard, b. 1860, who also died in infancy. It is curious that Ada was the only child who was given the name of Goodrich.

Mary Freer died at the age of forty-five, of tuberculosis, on 10th December 1862, so that at the age of five years Ada Goodrich Freer became motherless, in company with her four surviving brothers, Benjamin, George, Arthur, and Ernest. We may note in passing that a lady named Elizabeth Stokes, and not George Freer, was the informant of Mary's death to the registrar on 12th December 1862 having also been present at the death two days previously. In November 1863 Hannah, daughter of an Uppingham drover named John Cave, evidently became pregnant by the widowed George Freer. They were married on 20th March 1864 and their child Mary was born on 1st August, living only nine months. On 8th January 1866 a second child of this union, Howard, was born. His father survived him by a matter of days only, for George died on 21st January 1866 aged forty-six. Ada Goodrich Freer and her brothers had lost both father and mother in the space of little over four years.

The Freers were not well off, and indeed according to the Probate Registries in both London and Leicester, Miss Freer's parents left neither money nor real estate. The position of their five surviving children would not be an easy one, for it is reasonable to suppose that Hannah Freer, the drover's daughter, would be reluctant to take responsibility for the bringing-up of the children of the first wife of George Freer, to whom she had been married less than two years before his death.

It follows that Miss Freer's claim in her subsequent writings that she was 'brought up by an elderly relative with early Victorian standards'[1] could well be true, and is indeed confirmed in general terms by her niece, Mrs K. M. Connors, whom I located after not inconsiderable enquiry and correspondence. Mrs Connors, who was born in 1884, and is the daughter of Benjamin Freer, is the last

[1] Quoted from a contribution by Miss Freer to Edith K. Harper's *Stead: The Man*, London, 1918, p. 63.

surviving close relative I have been able to find after a protracted investigation in England, South Africa, and finally New Zealand, where Mrs Connors lives. She has told me that Benjamin Freer, who was seventeen when his father died, 'did his best to bring up his three brothers', presumably with help from local relatives. The responsibility for Ada's education and upbringing, however, was assumed by 'an aunt who had a boarding school for young ladies', but most unfortunately Mrs Connors never knew (or has forgotten) the name of this relative and the location of the school. It was not in or near Uppingham, and Mrs Connors believed that it was located in Yorkshire. She has told me that her parents never discussed 'Aunt Ada' because of 'family dislikes'. I have no doubt myself, on the evidence of Miss Freer's literary skill, that the 'elderly relative' did provide her with an excellent education.

Miss Freer was able to make a most favourable impression upon the eminent Victorians with whom by 1888 onwards she was in contact, mainly through the introduction of F. W. H. Myers, including Henry and Eleanor Sidgwick, Lord Bute, and others, because of her social accomplishments, charm, good looks, and curiously youthful appearance. There can be no doubt about her attractive personality. In 1888, when she was thirty-one, F. W. H. Myers wrote privately of her beautiful grey eyes and believed her to be in her middle twenties, as did W. T. Stead, who first met her in 1891 when she was thirty-four.[1] The Rev. Peter Dewar, in a letter to Lord Bute of 13th July 1894, remarked that her 'powers of sympathy seemed to me to be supernormal', while in the same year he referred with pleasure to Bute's own 'high opinion of her gifts and graces'. The enthusiastic first opinions of Alexander Carmichael, the distinguished author of *Carmina Gadelica*, and George Henderson, later Lecturer in Celtic at Glasgow University, expressed in letters from Carmichael to Fr Allan McDonald in August 1896, were similar.[2] That Miss Freer was aware of her attractions for the opposite sex is revealed by a comment in her letter to Lord Bute of 5th July 1895 about the difficulty of finding a woman companion for her second visit to the Highlands and the Isles as a result of her friend Miss Constance Moore's necessary attendance upon her invalid father. Miss Freer said that plenty of men would be glad to accompany her, but that Mrs Grundy would not permit it.

[1] F. Whyte, *Life of W. T. Stead*, vol. II, p. 38.
[2] Carmichael wrote that Henderson 'is charmed, as we all are, with Miss Freer', adding two weeks later that Fr Allan would soon be seeing her himself and that Carmichael heartily envied him. Miss Freer was nearly forty at this period, but looked very much younger.

I do not think that there can be any doubt that those she met, and so completely charmed, accepted her own assessment of her intellectual abilities and social and educational background. W. T. Stead, after his first meeting with her in 1891, wrote that she 'lives in Society, has had a first-class education, and is perfectly self-possessed'.[1] Two years later, when he was announcing the publication of *Borderland*, he amplified this opinion and quoted the views of others:

I should not have attempted the publication of this quarterly had I not been fortunate enough to secure the assistance and collaboration of a lady who, of all others, is most competent to execute my idea. For some years past every reader of the Proceedings of the Psychical Research Society has been well aware of the contributions of a lady who in the papers is always referred to as Miss X. In all the investigations of the Society into the phenomena of telepathy, crystal-vision and shell-hearing, together with many other departments of research, Miss X constantly appears and re-appears as one of the most trustworthy, careful and exact of all their inquirers. Her papers on crystal-vision are the classic upon the subject, for Miss X was the pioneer of the Society in this most promising field of research. This has been repeatedly recognized both at home and abroad by the leading authorities. M. Janet, for instance, who is probably the most eminent of French investigators into psychical phenomena, told the International Congress of Experimental Psychology, which met in London in 1892, that his attention was first turned to the subject of crystal-vision by reading Miss X's papers, and he cordially attested the exactitude and importance of her observations. Herr Max Dessoir, writing in the Monist, *declared that Miss X 'possesses a highly critical mind, is well acquainted with the common sources of error in this department of investigation, and her testimony is, in his [sic] opinion, more valuable than that of all the early authors put together'. Miss X is a lady of good birth and education, familiar to her finger-tips with almost all the phases of the phenomena under consideration, and capable of following the evidence and arguments in three or four laguages. I am extremely glad that the publication of* Borderland *promises to supply a sphere in which the exceptional talents and rare natural gifts of Miss X may be utilized to the best advantages for the purpose of psychical research.*[2]

It was perhaps inappropriate for Miss Freer herself to quote, as she did, a letter from an acquaintance describing her as 'refined, edu-

[1] *Life of W. T. Stead*, vol. II, p. 38.
[2] *Review of Reviews*, 1893, vol. VII, p. 678.

cated, and well-connected',[1] but there can be little doubt that this was the public image of herself she had created. Much had happened to her since her days in Uppingham, days that she was evidently anxious to conceal for the rest of her life.

Who was the 'fairy godmother' who gave Miss Freer these advantages? And if Mrs Connors' memories of what happened many years ago are well founded, where was the school for young ladies that was the source of Miss Freer's excellent education and social graces? One thing seems certain, and that is that Miss Freer was just as determined to conceal the identity of the elderly relative and her school as she was anxious to hide the modest circumstances of her birth in Uppingham. It would have been simple and becoming for her to state the facts, instead of imposing upon her readers the mass of vague hints with which her writings are so liberally embellished, to the exclusion of even the smallest fragment of definite information. She could so easily and generously have said, 'After the death of both my parents I was brought up by my aunt, Miss So-and-so, who had a school for girls at So-and-so, and to whom I shall be indebted all my life for the advantage of a very good education.' She never did. The reader may think that a probable reason for this secretiveness is that the kindly relative who did so much for the orphaned Ada Freer did not measure up to the social background which, by 1888, she wished her new friends in the oligarchy of the Society for Psychical Research to associate with her. It seems probable that the country house with its grooms and gardeners, the supposed scene of her upbringing, existed only in her imagination, like her Scottish descent.

I think it likely that her complementary pose in print as 'a woman of leisure'[2] and independent wealth was also assumed. Certainly she was not possessed of any private fortune, for when she died the value of her estate was sworn as less than $1,000 by her husband. In the early 1890s she was seeking paid employment from both W. T. Stead and the Swanley Horticultural College, very privately advertising her services in occult matters,[3] and at the same time obtaining

---

[1] *Essays in Psychical Research*, p. 188.

[2] *Transactions of the Gaelic Society of Inverness*, 1896, vol. XXI, p. 110. This was clearly untrue on the basis of her appointment as the paid assistant editor of the spiritualist paper *Borderland* alone. She received a salary of £200 per annum from W. T. Stead, the proprietor, which was not insubstantial remuneration for a woman at the end of the nineteenth century.

[3] I do not think there can be any doubt that the advertiser in the first volume of *Borderland*, from the address of the private office used by Miss Freer in Pall Mall East and describing herself as 'A Lady with considerable psychical experience', with 'Terms on Application', was Miss Freer.

loans on occasions from Stead and Lord Bute. The mystery presented by her monetary affairs, however, is that for a year or two prior to this her position seems to have been quite different. In the late 1880s, when she was closely associated with F. W. H. Myers, she was living, apparently alone in London, at St Stephen's Ladies' Home in Westbourne Grove Terrace, ostensibly without any need to earn her living. For a period she seemed to be able to devote unlimited time to experimenting with automatic writing, crystal-gazing, and similar subjects, under the guidance of Myers, and to preparing long papers on these matters, which Myers read to the S.P.R. and published in the *Proceedings*, while strictly preserving the anonymity of the writer. Miss Freer said that she did the work on at least one of these papers while actually staying in the house of Myers' elderly mother. From this it would seem either that Myers was privately supporting his protégée until about 1891, when he recommended her to W. T. Stead as a paid literary assistant and later as the assistant editor of *Borderland*, or that she had some private source of income which ceased after a few years. Certainly money became a matter of serious importance to her from the early 1890s onwards, and it is noteworthy that by 1895 she had become a permanent guest at the house of her friend, Miss Constance Moore, with whom she was to live until she left England in 1901.

A point in favour of these arguments is that enquiry has not resulted in the discovery of any 'elderly relative' of Miss Freer who might be presumed to be socially distinguished or wealthy. Due to the kindness and diligence of the Rector of Uppingham, Canon S. C. Woodward, and the Deputy Superintendent Registrar of Uppingham District, Mrs Rosalie M. Russell, very full searches have been made among the records of the local families of Freer, Goodrich, and Adcock for an aunt of Miss Freer who could possess these qualifications, but without success.

The essential details of the Uppingham Freers have already been studied. Thomas Goodrich, like William Freer, was a wheelwright, and both he and his wife Elizabeth died in Uppingham without any recorded issue other than their daughter Ann, Ada's paternal grandmother. Josiah Adcock, a butcher who died in 1860, and his wife Ann, Ada's maternal grandparents, had only two daughters of whom particulars are recorded in Uppingham and its environs; Mary, Ada's mother, who married George Freer, and her sister Charlotte, who died unmarried in 1848 at the age of twenty-seven. So far as I have been able to ascertain, the line of Uppingham Adcocks ceased in 1862. Ann Adcock, widow of Josiah, died on 2nd November of that year, while Mary Freer died a few weeks later on 10th December.

Faced with these failures, an attempt has been made to pinpoint the district where the 'aunt' and her school might have been located, by examining the allusions to her childhood days with which Miss Freer's writings are plentifully sprinkled. Experience has shown that these reminiscences must be read with reservations. Miss Freer wrote, for example:

It was my privilege when a child in the schoolroom to spend an occasional half-holiday in very good company. The Carlyles were there, and lively little Miss Jewsbury, and many others whom I would fain remember and whom I should better appreciate in these latter days, for in sooth, I then thought them all noisy and mostly shrill, and as the Sunday afternoons wore away in talk which I but little understood, the chances dwindled of my being taken to hear the music at St Mark's, Chelsea, and, after all, I liked that best—that and the artist who drew pictures for me. I have some of them now, and I hope he is at least a Royal Academician by this time, though as they are not signed and I forget his name, I shall not profit by his promotion![1]

Jane Welsh Carlyle died in 1866, so that this charming story, suggesting that Miss Freer was acquainted during Mrs Carlyle's lifetime with the social and literary scene in London, would by itself contradict her various claims to have been born in 1865, 1870, and 1874. As she was born in 1857, however, it could have been true, and we have to consider it despite Mrs Connors' belief that Miss Freer was educated in Yorkshire, with which this account is at variance. Thomas and Jane Carlyle were, of course, established in Cheyne Row, Chelsea, many years before the death of Mrs Carlyle, so that it will be seen that Miss Freer's story of those pleasant afternoons spent in their company during her half-holidays from the schoolroom, if true, would place her early upbringing and education by her relative, in London. I am inclined to think, however, that this single reference to London as the location was pure invention, for it is confirmed neither by Mrs Connors nor by the rest of Miss Freer's colourful asides on this subject, the latter being reasonably consistent. She wrote, for example, in connexion with her capacity for crystal-gazing, discovered and developed under the guidance of F. W. H. Myers, that 'as a child far away in the north' she used to climb from rock to rock until she reached a moorland tarn in which she could see visions of distant lands and water-maidens with beckoning hands, and referred to 'the accident of a north-country upbringing'.[2] She said that she had lived from her earliest years

[1] *Borderland*, 1893–4, vol. I, p. 117.
[2] A. Goodrich-Freer, 'Hobson Jobson', *Nineteenth Century*, April 1902, p. 585.

'among the people of a northern village'.[1] In her introduction to an edition of Susan Ferrier's novels that she published in 1902 she referred to herself as 'we of the north'. It is clear that these allusions (and especially to the moorland tarn) could not apply to London or to the gentle, pastoral contours of Rutland in the English Midlands. If they meant anything at all, they referred to the location of her upbringing and education by her relative during the period of her schooldays, from about 1866, when she became an orphan, to probably the mid-1870s.

It may, of course, be urged that Miss Freer was such a proven fabricator of stories about herself that any endeavour to make sense of these pointers is like trying to follow the trail of a fish in water. On the other hand, her repeated claims to have been brought up in the north have some slight independent support from a comment by Frederic Whyte in his book on W. T. Stead. Whyte said that in 1891 'an old friend of Stead's, the Rev. Henry Kendal [sic] of Darlington' told Stead that Miss Freer, whom he knew well, was 'a depository of endless stores of authentic information as to apparitions'.[2] Henry Kendall was, of course, the minister of the Darlington Congregational Church from 1859 to 1893. Darlington is in Durham, just over the boundary with Yorkshire. Mrs Connors' memory of what happened to Miss Freer, moreover, seems to me to be confirmed up to a point by two facts that are established. The research in Uppingham has shown that Miss Freer was an orphan by 1866 and was, therefore, not brought up by her parents, while the quality of her literary work indicates her standard of education. It may be said, too, that while her anxiety to ingratiate herself with the wealthy Lord Bute offered an obvious motive for her claim to an 'inherited Highland sympathy with the mysterious', as it was styled in her obituary,[3] it is not apparent what she had to gain by stating that she had been brought up in the north of England if this was not true.

Other stories by Miss Freer suggest that her more general references to the north could be narrowed to Yorkshire, and indeed to the West Riding. When she was emphasizing her extreme suitability for the Scottish Second Sight Enquiry to Lord Bute and the Rev. Peter Dewar in 1894 she said (somewhat loftily, it might be thought) that she was accustomed to the Yorkshire peasantry, and that her patron could, therefore, assume that she would know exactly how to deal with the people of the Highlands and the Isles. In an unpublished letter to Lord Bute of 17th January 1896 she said that her

---

[1] *Borderland*, 1895, vol. II, pp. 263-4.
[2] *The Life of W. T. Stead*, vol. II, p. 38.
[3] *Folklore*, 1931, vol. XLI, p. 299.

Yorkshire home was 'in the heart of the Quaker country'.[1] She
evidently knew York Minster sufficiently well to refer to it very
appropriately as 'overwhelming',[2] and she was familiar enough with
Yorkshire terms to refer to the 'Boggarts of Yorkshire'.[3] She wrote
of an old country house in the Vale of York with which she was
familiar.[4] She referred to the 'welcome West Riding accents' of a
chance acquaintance,[5] and spoke of second sight 'in the West Riding
of Yorkshire' in a lecture to the Scottish Society of Literature and
Art in 1901.[6] There were also two references at least by Miss Freer,
vague though they were, to country dominated by hills and moors.
One of these occurred in her lecture reported in the *Oban Times*
already quoted, while her description of herself 'as a child far away
in the north', climbing from rock to rock until she reached a
moorland tarn, will be remembered.

Finally, in an article 'Folklore and Psychical Research', in which
she answered some criticisms of the S.P.R. made by Mr Edward
Clodd in his presidential address to the Folklore Society in 1895,
Miss Freer described her 'northern village'. She wrote:

*I admit some prejudice on my part, having been, according to my lights,
a folk-lorist from my earliest years, the natural result of living among
the people of a northern village, rich in tradition and story, where
mumming plays were of triennial occurrence, and Dolmens and Menhirs,
and Roll-right stones, and rocks with cup-markings, and Celtic inscriptions, and Roman altars, and Saxon crosses, were things of every
day.*

*Can I not to this day quote pages of Racine, and Pearson on the
Creed, and dreary 'sacred' poetry learnt in bitter punishment for happy,
never-to-be-forgotten hours, when perched in an apple-tree or on a
manger, I drank in from groom and gardener many a story of local
witches and boggarts and rocking stones and cromlechs?*[7]

---

[1] While the early strength of the Quaker movement in Yorkshire cannot be
disputed (see W. C. Braithwaite, *The Beginnings of Quakerism*, London, 1923,
pp. 368–70), there is, in my view, no special area of the county where the
Quakers established themselves above all others. There were important groups
in most of the larger towns of the West Riding, such as Leeds, Huddersfield,
Halifax, and Wakefield. Bradford was a considerable stronghold (A. R. Hodgson,
The Society of Friends in Bradford. A Record of 270 Years, Bradford, 1926). So,
also, was York, where the great Quaker families engaged in the manufacture of
chocolate wielded considerable influence. The Quaker public school at Ack-
worth is near Pontefract, in the south of the West Riding.
[2] *Essays in Psychical Research*, p. 42.
[3] *Ibid.*, p. 80. [4] *Ibid.*, p. 93. [5] *Ibid.*, p. 280.
[6] *Oban Times*, 23rd November 1901.
[7] *Borderland*, 1895, vol. II, pp. 263–4.

It could be argued that this collection of asides by Miss Freer may well be deliberately misleading and therefore valueless, and that in any event the location of her upbringing and education is not of sufficient importance to justify any serious speculation on the basis of the available information. On the other hand, it seems to me that however purposefully imprecise Miss Freer undoubtedly was in her references to a West Riding upbringing, these allusions do at least form a sufficiently consistent pattern of informed half-truths to merit some consideration. I confess, moreover, that to anyone interested in the antiquities of Yorkshire, her description of her 'northern village' can hardly fail to be of great interest and worthy of some examination.

It is noteworthy that after her single quoted reference in 1895 to the folklore and antiquities of her 'northern village' Miss Freer never again discussed in print the origin of her early interest in such matters, so far as I am aware. This is surprising, for she wrote voluminously and professionally on these subjects in subsequent years. It might be thought that the village of her upbringing, 'rich in tradition and story', would have provided a familiar, convenient, and immediate field for description and personal comment by so able a writer as Miss Freer. There must, it would seem, have been some good reason why the scenes of her later writings on folklore and kindred subjects in Great Britain were limited to the Highlands and the Islands of Scotland, which she knew only from her several brief visits for psychical research purposes, with the added disadvantage that she was unacquainted with Gaelic. As her picture of her 'northern village' was undoubtedly overdrawn, it is possible that some of her more obvious errors were drawn to her attention, causing her embarrassment and a resultant decision that it would be prudent not to refer to the subject again.

One of Miss Freer's more patent mistakes was to claim that there were 'Roll-right stones' in her village in the north. These curiosities are, of course, specifically the circle of stones three to five feet high near the villages of Great and Little Rollright in Oxfordshire.[1] Another glaring error was her reference to mumming plays 'of triennial occurrence', which are non-existent. The leading authority on this subject, Mr Alex Helm, a member of the Council of the Folklore Society, further informs me that the only truly traditional

---

[1] For a description of the Rollright stones see James Fergusson, *Rude Stone Monuments in all Countries*, London, 1872, pp. 124–6. They are illustrated in a photograph opposite p. 168 of J. Cannan's *Oxfordshire*, London, 1952. See also A. J. Evans, M.A., F.S.A., 'The Rollright Stones and their Folklore', *Folklore*, March, 1895, pp. 5–51.

ceremony in the country celebrated every third year is the painting and re-raising of the village maypole at Barwick-in-Elmet,[1] only a few miles from the 'northern village' of Thorner in the West Riding of Yorkshire where I lived for many years.

In assessing the worth of Miss Freer's description of the scene of her upbringing, expert help has been available to me from an old friend, the late Hartley Thwaite, J.P., F.S.A., of the Yorkshire Archaeological Society, who has confirmed that her effusive account, with its plethora of antiquities, cannot apply accurately to any single known location in the British Isles. The extreme rarity of Celtic inscriptions, I am informed, enables these to be pinpointed geographically with precision. They do not exist anywhere to our present knowledge in company with the multiplicity of the other types of historic remains, described by Miss Freer as 'things of every day'. Her mention of the Celtic inscriptions and the Rollright stones is sufficient to indicate that her knowledge of archaeology was very superficial.

If Miss Freer's description is considered tolerantly, however, ignoring the more flagrant mistakes I have mentioned and making due allowance for her somewhat vivid imagination and lack of expertise, it is of great interest to anyone familiar, even in the most amateur sense, with the archaeological history of Yorkshire. It seemed to me, too, that if the account of the 'northern village' had any truth in it, the problem of locating it could be approached in an alternative way. If Mrs Connors' recollection was accurate so far as it went, directories of the period might contain a record of the school for young ladies existing in the 1860s, when Miss Freer's aunt assumed the responsibility for her upbringing. In following this tenuous clue, I had no choice but to assume that the school-owning aunt was unmarried and that her name was Freer, or in the alternative either Adcock or Goodrich, these latter being the maiden names of Miss Freer's mother and grandmother.

Miss Freer's description at first seemed to me possibly to point to the village of Aldborough, near Boroughbridge, on the boundary of the West and North Ridings of Yorkshire. Certainly no other

---

[1] Rev. F. S. Colman, *A History of the Parish of Barwick-in-Elmet in the County of York*, Leeds, 1908, pp. 19–25. Miss Freer could not have been describing Barwick-in-Elmet, for this village, while proud of a remarkable and extensive series of ancient earth-works, possesses none of the antiquities listed by her and is situated in level pastoral country. It is an odd coincidence that Thomas Dykes, the grandfather of Dr John Bacchus Dykes mentioned in the previous chapter, was briefly curate of Barwick-in-Elmet in 1789–91 (*ibid.*, p. 86) before becoming vicar of St John's Church, Hull. The Dykes had no later connexion with Barwick-in-Elmet.

village in this part of England contains more of the features mentioned by Miss Freer. Aldborough was the Iseur of the ancient Britons and the Isurium of the Romans. From the point of view of a person writing in London, Aldborough is certainly 'a northern village, rich in tradition and story'.[1] There is both a Saxon cross and a Roman altar there. The most striking point of identification, however, is the presence, a mile away, of the three menhirs, or 'Devil's Arrows', situated in two fields in Boroughbridge. These three monoliths vary from eighteen to twenty-two feet in height, and archaeologists seem uncertain whether they are of British or Roman origin. Menhirs in groups like these[2] are exceedingly rare, and indeed the only other menhir in Yorkshire known to me is the single example at Rudston, a village in the East Riding near the coastal town of Bridlington. Neither Roman altars nor Saxon crosses are plentiful, and the occurrence at Aldborough of these curiosities close to the well-known 'Devil's Arrows' is probably unique, and is certainly so in the north of England. On the other hand, Aldborough is situated in flat pastoral country. There are no moorland tarns.

Aldborough has been visited. It would have been very pleasant to pin down Miss Freer's childhood village to this discovery, but an investigation has not been fruitful. Some temporary interest was aroused by the discovery that Henry Goodricke was the vicar of Aldborough from 1750 to 1801, but he left no descendants of whom there are any records in the district. The vicar of Aldborough, Rev. S. A. Atherley, has most kindly searched his records for me, as has his colleague at Boroughbridge, but without result. Reference books and directories of the period give some details of the inhabitants of Aldborough and Boroughbridge and of private schools, but unfortunately the names of Goodrich, Freer, and Adcock are conspicuous by their absence.

The ancient village of Adel, near Leeds, now almost a suburb of Yorkshire's largest city, qualified on some points, for it possesses the remains of three Roman altars and some notable Saxon anti-

---

[1] T. S. Turner, in his *History of Aldborough and Boroughbridge, Containing an Account of the Roman Antiquities, Devil's Arrows, Churches, Halls and Other Curiosities*, London, 1853, says that there are few places in England where one can enjoy the historical past with greater pleasure than the village of Aldborough, while it is said in *The Tourist's Companion*, Ripon, 1818, that Aldborough has always arrested the attention and engaged the particular notice of antiquaries.

[2] Not to be confused with cromlechs, which are not uncommon in Yorkshire. Menhirs, literally 'Long stones', are monumental standing stones of substantial height.

quities.[1] Although it was interesting to discover that Isaac Freer of Arthington, a nearby village, is buried at Adel,[2] it soon became clear that this could not be Miss Freer's 'northern village'. Isaac died on 24th March 1696 and is the last Freer recorded in Adel. Directories of the period showed no school that fitted, and Adel has no menhirs or moorland tarns.

Ilkley, an inland resort of great beauty on the river Wharfe, with fine moorland scenery, was the Olicana of the Romans. It has three carved Saxon crosses in the churchyard. Its present population of some 19,000 started to grow from small beginnings in the middle of the nineteenth century, with the advent of the railways. Less than 500 people lived there in the first half of that century,[3] and it was still being described as a village in Kelly's *Post Office Directory of the West Riding of Yorkshire* in the 1860s and 1870s.

In their great book on Ilkley[4] Dr R. Collyer and J. H. Turner describe the antiquities to be found on Rombalds Moor (popularly called Ilkley Moor) which immediately adjoins the southern outskirts of the town. These included 'cup-marked rocks' and a 'despoiled rocking stone and cromlech'.[5] The 'circle, sixteen yards in diameter, composed of twelve upright stones, three or four feet high',[6] known as the Twelve Apostles, might have been mistaken by the uninformed Miss Freer for menhirs, as might 'Cowper's Cross', an upright stone modernly (in 1868) fashioned into a Calvary Cross,[7] or the 'two pyramidal idol rocks, and a rock bearing cup marks on the margin',[8] on the highest part of the moor. There are, in addition, barrows, pit dwellings, burial mounds, cairns, and other relics on Rombalds Moor.

The Roman altar discovered at Ilkley is illustrated on p. 17 of *Ilkley: Ancient and Modern*, while the three ancient Saxon crosses now in Ilkley churchyard are shown on p. 41. The reader may think,

[1] See Henry T. Simpson, *Archaelogia Adelensia, or a History of the Parish of Adel*, London, 1879, and George Lewthwaite, *Adel: Its Norman Church . . . and Other Early Antiquities*, Lincoln, Leeds, and London, 1887.

[2] *The Registers of the Parish Church of Adel* (*Publications of the Thoresby Society*), Leeds, 1895, vol. V, p. 128. Mr Vincent Sternberg, one of the principal actors in the ghostly drama of the Leeds Library, discussed in my *New Light on Old Ghosts*, is buried at Adel.

[3] Thomas Allen, *A New and Complete History of the County of York*, London, 1832, vol. VI, p. 143.

[4] Robert Collyer and J. Horsfall Turner, *Ilkley: Ancient and Modern*, Otley, 1885.

[5] *Ibid.*, p. lxxx.   [6] *Ibid.*, p. lxxxiii.

[7] The authors were quoting from a pamphlet printed in Wakefield in 1868, *Rambles on Rombalds Moor*, by C. Forrest and W. Grainge.

[8] *Ibid.*, p. lxxxiv.

against the background of the reservations to which I have drawn attention in previous pages, that there are some quite striking correspondences between Ilkley as it was in the nineteenth century and Miss Freer's description of her 'northern village'. Moorland tarns are shown on both ancient and modern maps of Ilkley, and some of these are in quite close proximity to the town.

While the archaeological enquiry was being pursued, *Kelly's Post Office Directory of the West Riding of Yorkshire* was searched, and disclosed the very interesting information that a Miss Ann Adcock had a private boarding school for girls in Ilkley from 1861 to about the middle of the 1870s. I could trace no other entry of a private boarding school for girls in the whole of the West Riding in the name of Freer, Adcock, or Goodrich.

Kelly's *Directory* gave no address for Miss Adcock's establishment for young ladies. Slater's *Royal National Commercial Directory of the County of York*, 1864, however, gave the school as being situated at Ilkley Hall. Local guide-books of the period[1] were examined at Ilkley, together with Shuttleworth's *New Map of Ilkley*, 1874. These, together with the 1875 issue of Slater's *Directory* at the British Museum, provided some additional information.

The 1863 edition of Shuttleworth, under 'Boarding Schools for Young Ladies', listed Miss Adcock's establishment as being at The Hall, Ilkley, while the 1865 issue gave the location as Bilberry Bank, Crossbeck Road. Slater showed the address as Ilkley Hall in 1864, and Crossbeck Road in 1875. Denton gave the Bilberry Bank address in his local guide-book in 1871. This information showed that Miss Adcock moved her school in or about 1864, some two years before Miss Freer became an orphan, from Ilkley Hall, a sizeable property in its own grounds and an impressive address for a boarding school, to Bilberry Bank, a much smaller semi-detached house with a steeply sloping garden backing directly on to the moor[2] in those days.

This sounds very much as if Miss Adcock's young lady pupils were diminishing in numbers by 1864, which is rather confirmed by the fact that the last record of the school's existence is in the issue of Slater published in 1875, when it seems to have finally closed down altogether. The reason for the school losing ground and the move to much smaller premises may well have been increased competition

---

[1] Notably *Shuttleworth's Guide-book to Ilkley and Vicinity*, published at Ilkley in 1863, with a second edition in 1865, and *Denton's Ilkley Directory, Guide Book and Almanac*, Ilkley, 1871.

[2] Bilberry Bank and the adjoining house Moorlands (the names are very descriptive of the situation) are shown on the map of 1874, but no longer exist today.

from rival schools being established in Ilkley at this period, due to the very suitable situation for girls' boarding schools of this beautiful and healthful district. Shuttleworth, in the second edition of his guide-book, listed three other schools similar to that of Miss Adcock, all in the same part of Ilkley.

If the reader considers that it is probable that Miss Ann Adcock was the 'elderly relative', and that Miss Freer's schooldays were indeed spent among the Saxon crosses, the rocks with cup-markings, the rocking stones and cromlechs, the stone circles, Roman altars, and moorland tarns of Ilkley, then he may think that the other indications, already discussed, that Miss Freer had no background of wealth are rather confirmed by what little we know of Miss Adcock and her school. Miss Freer's parents had no money, and it would seem that the 'elderly relative', if she was Miss Adcock, was not possessed of any substantial means. This opinion is supported by the results of another line of enquiry.

I asked an old schoolfellow, Mr John Lancaster, of the West Riding Registry of Deeds, if he would look at his records during the relevant period. He kindly did so, and after an extensive search had to report that the name of Ann Adcock does not appear at all in his indexes of Ilkley. As registration of all property transactions was compulsory in the West Riding in the latter part of the nineteenth century, this means that Miss Adcock was the owner of neither Ilkley Hall nor Bilberry Bank, and that as leases of twenty-one years and more were also required to be registered, it follows that her tenancies were only of short duration, as is indicated by the facts previously assembled. Miss Adcock was not a property owner.

Another interesting discovery is that Miss Adcock was not a member of any old-established Ilkley family. The name Adcock does not appear at all in William Cooper's *The Parish Registers of Ilkley, 1597–1812*, which was privately printed in 1927 for the Yorkshire Parish Register Society, nor was Miss Adcock recorded as a resident of Ilkley in the directories to which reference has already been made, except for the period when she had her school. This suggests that she came to the small community of Ilkley from some other part of England shortly before 1860, which would make it possible for her to have been a member of the Adcock family resident in the Leicestershire, Northamptonshire, and Rutland district at that time.

What happened to Miss Adcock when she gave up her school in the mid-1870s is a mystery which I have not been able to solve.[1]

[1] One reason why we know so little about Miss Adcock's school is that it is not mentioned, either by advertisement or in any other way, in any issue of *The Ilkley Gazette* during the relevant period.

Miss Margaret E. Hutchin, the Superintendent Registrar of the Wharfedale Registration District, has most kindly established for me that Miss Adcock neither married nor died in this part of Yorkshire during the last thirty years of the nineteenth century. My colleague Mr H. E. Pratt has spent many diligent Saturday mornings at Somerset House going completely through the whole of the indexes throughout the same period over the whole country with the same object. Some forty certificates of deaths or marriages have been taken out and examined, quite apart from the scrutiny of other entries in the indexes relating to Ann Adcocks who could be ruled out on account of impossible ages, such as those in their teens or eighties when the school was established about 1860. A large proportion of the deceased Ann Adcocks were, of course, married women who did not qualify. It is disappointing, however, that among those remaining we could discover no Ann Adcock who was described as a retired schoolmistress, or who could be convincingly identified with Miss Adcock of Ilkley. It would have been very agreeable to complete this small fringe investigation in a definite and satisfying way, but so far we have not been able to do so with any degree of confidence. As I have remarked to Dr Campbell on more than one occasion, Miss Adcock seems to have obliterated her trail almost as successfully as Miss Freer. She may or may not have been the 'elderly relative', and my hope is that this book may conceivably come to the notice of somebody who can supply the essential information for which we have looked for so long, and which Miss Freer could have given in a single sentence had she thought fit to do so.[1]

As Miss Freer was born in 1857, she would be eighteen in 1875, when her schooldays may be presumed to have been over. How was her time spent between 1875 and the later 1880s, when she was living in London, came under the notice of F. W. H. Myers, and ultimately joined the S.P.R.? We cannot answer this question with any certainty, because we have no information beyond a variety of vague statements made by Miss Freer herself which may or may not be true. Many of these comments are contained in her long anonymous paper, 'A Record of Telepathic and Other Experiences',[2] read to the S.P.R. for her by F. W. H. Myers on 25th October 1889. If the

[1] One can only speculate whether Ann Adcock may have been the 'old lady in the spirit wearing a cap who is fond of you—your grandmother' whom Mrs Piper described to Miss Freer in a séance on 7th December 1889, and whom Mrs Piper said was 'named Anne'. Miss Freer said this was a correct description of a friend whom she was 'in the habit of calling Granny' (*Borderland*, I, 227).

[2] *Proceedings*, S.P.R., 1889–90, vol. VI, pp. 358–97.

'elderly relative' was still alive she does not seem to have taken much part in Miss Freer's reminiscences of her life during this period.

She stayed, she said, 'in a country vicarage in the North', at a date unstated, where the children of the house were her constant play-fellows (p. 371), while in 1875 she was a guest in 'a country house in the Midland counties' (p. 372). She enjoyed supernormal experiences during both these visits, which seems to have been her invariable habit wherever she went.

On p. 363 of her paper she said that when she was a child of thirteen she was taken to see a college, to which it was proposed to send her later to complete her studies. She saw an apparition in an empty classroom (it was during the vacation period), and when in later years she took her place in the college she met a girl whom she called 'N', the original of the apparition, and established a friendship with her 'which has never changed'. If this story is true, it may be that Miss Freer's education continued until 1878 or so, when she was twenty-one. Who 'N' was, I do not know. If we bring ourselves to believe Miss Freer to a limited degree, it cannot have been her devoted friend Miss Constance Moore, for according to Miss Freer's letter to Fr Allan McDonald of 28th October 1901, she and Miss Moore had been 'twenty-one years together', which would mean that their intimate friendship did not start until 1880.

On the assumption that Miss Freer's paper was not entirely fiction, it seems to me that Miss Moore must have been 'D', a friend with whom Miss Freer was staying in a country house in 1882, where the latter had a remarkable premonition (p. 374), although 'D' does not seem to have been her companion when Miss Freer was staying at another 'house in the country' in August 1887 (p. 372), nor when she was living 'in a private boarding-house' in August 1885, recovering from an illness and accompanied by someone (the elderly relative?) who was too deaf to hear passing conversation. Miss Freer said (p. 358) that 'during the last few years' she had formed an 'intimate friendship' with 'D', and that between their two minds telepathic communications occurred with such frequency that they had come to regard them as a matter of course.[1] She added (p. 362) that as 'D' had scarcely any other psychical experiences, this success probably depended upon their propinquity and

---

[1] It must be recorded, however, that in a letter to Lord Bute of 25th January 1896 Miss Freer said that Miss Moore 'scorns the whole subject' of psychical research. Mr (later Sir) John Ritchie Findlay, in a letter to Lord Bute of 3rd March 1897, describing his experiences during his stay at Ballechin House, said that 'Miss Moore, on the other hand, struck me as being a person of sound common sense, and her evidence I should value beyond that of all the others, who are pre-disposed by temperament to such experiences.'

common interests. For three months of the year 1888 Miss Freer stated that she and 'D' were living under the same roof (p. 377), and from the description of other incidents they seem to have lived within very easy reach of one another during the remainder of that year. In January 1889, moreover, the two friends were living together again, for Miss Freer described how they were reading their letters together which had just been delivered, and she was able to surprise 'D' by divining correctly the Christian name of the latter's correspondent as 'Wilhelmina', by seeing this in 'letters of light' against a dark background near the fireplace (p. 365). All this clearly suggests that if Miss Freer and Miss Moore had been 'twenty-one years together' in 1901, then Miss Moore and 'D' were one and the same person. Certainly they were together from 1895 onwards, when Miss Freer moved into Miss Moore's home, Holy Trinity Vicarage, Paddington, the house of the latter's father, the Rev. Daniel Moore.

It is for the reader to decide what credence he attaches to Miss Freer's accounts of her life as a young woman, which included a statement in 1894 that some time prior to 1890 she had been living with friends in Baltimore.[1] This occurred in a curious story which to me at least (surprisingly in the case of Miss Freer's writings) is not easy to follow. It concerned the psychometry of a cat's hair, a young woman with 'terrible headaches', and the alleged death of an elderly aunt of the family with whom Miss Freer was staying. All this is vague and unsatisfactory of course, and we are not really on firm ground until January 1888, when Miss Freer joined the S.P.R. We know that by then Miss Freer was living in London at St Stephen's Ladies' Home, and that this address remained unchanged in successive lists of members for some years. She certainly stayed for periods in other people's houses, including the home of the elderly mother of F. W. H. Myers, but St Stephen's Ladies' Home seems to have been her permanent address.

The foregoing pages do not seek to show that Miss Freer did not enjoy a more advantageous upbringing than her brothers whom she left behind in Uppingham. I think that there is no doubt that she did. What has been demonstrated, I venture to think, is that her secretiveness and her addiction to misleading statements about herself, which she continued to display virtually to her death, enabled her to conceal the details of much of her life very effectively indeed. More importantly, the reader may think that attention has been

[1] *Borderland*, January, 1894, vol. I, p. 229. But it is just possible that this story though quoted by Miss Freer in the first person, relates an experience of someone else, who is not named.

drawn to material by which we can estimate the likely truth of Miss Freer's stories of her psychical experiences, which occupied so many pages of the *Proceedings* of the S.P.R., and enabled her quite rapidly to become a leading member of that organization at an important period in its history.

3

MISS FREER AND THE S.P.R.

AFTER EDMUND GURNEY, a man of brilliance and complete integrity, had taken his life in a Brighton hotel in June 1888,[1] his work as Honorary Secretary of the S.P.R. was taken over jointly by Frederic W. H. Myers and Frank Podmore. It is hard to avoid the melancholy conclusion that with Gurney's critical counsel silenced by his death, there was a deterioration in the standards of evidence adopted by the leaders of the Society in the cases they printed in their *Proceedings*. In July 1889, for example, F. W. H. Myers published, as a genuine case of haunting, the story of the Leeds Library ghost,[2] without disclosing that in January and February of the same year he had received letters from two of the principal witnesses which threw the gravest doubts upon the whole affair.[3] The suppression of these two letters was repeated in 1903, when the Leeds Library case was reprinted without amendment in Myers' book, published after his death.[4] Those familiar with the work and

---

[1] After *The Strange Case of Edmund Gurney* appeared in 1964, some additional evidence from the past became available, supporting my theory that Gurney's suicide was concealed by the S.P.R. leaders. *The Diary of Alice James*, originally privately printed in four copies in 1894, was published in 1965 with an introduction by Dr L. Edel. Alice James was the sister of William and Henry James. William James was a friend of Gurney, Myers, and Sidgwick and became President of the S.P.R. On 5th August 1889, shortly after William James had arrived in England, Miss James wrote in her diary, 'They say there is little doubt that Mr Edmund Gurney committed suicide. What a pity to hide it; every educated person who kills himself does something towards lessening the superstition' (1965 edition, p. 52).

[2] F. W. H. Myers, 'On Recognised Apparitions Occurring More than a Year After Death', *Proceedings*, S.P.R. 1889-90, vol. VI, pp. 13-65.

[3] The two letters concerned, written to Myers by Mr (later Sir) John Y. W. Macalister and the Rev. Charles Hargrove, are still in the files of the S.P.R. Their surprising contents are discussed in my *New Light on Old Ghosts*, London, 1965, pp. 35-53.

[4] *Human Personality and Its Survival of Bodily Death*, London, 1903, vol. II, pp. 380-1. The book was edited by Dr Richard Hodgson and Miss Alice Johnson, two prominent members of the S.P.R. Another example of Miss Johnson's concealment of evidence, that of her pamphlet on the Smith/Blackburn 'mind-reading' fiasco, printed in 1909, is documented and discussed in my book on Edmund Gurney.

character of Edmund Gurney may think that such a concealment of vital facts would not have occurred when he was Honorary Secretary of the Society and editor of its *Proceedings*.[1]

Miss Freer became prominent in the affairs of the S.P.R. during this period of increasing credulity on the part of its leaders, and what seems, indeed, to have been their determination to prove at all costs the existence and reality of psychic phenomena. The climate of the Society could hardly have been more appropriate for the enthusiastic reception and publication of Miss Freer's engaging accounts of her childhood visions, her crystal-gazing, and her telepathic experiences in the unnamed country houses and rectories in which she claimed to have stayed. The fact that not a shred of corroborative evidence, nor even of identification of places and persons, was offered in connexion with any of these wonders meant that the stories could be published without fear of them being checked, with a consequent precipitation of the kind of disaster that had followed the earlier printing of cases like that of Sir Edmund Hornby.[2] This affair, in which the Society had unfortunately given names and dates, had been exposed, after publication, as such nonsense that the S.P.R. had no choice but to withdraw the part of the volume of *Proceedings* in which the Hornby case had been included, and issue a reprint with another story substituted, occupying exactly the same amount of space.

There can be no doubt that from first joining the Society in 1888, Miss Freer made a most favourable impression upon the oligarchy of the S.P.R. Professor Henry Sidgwick, one of the Society's founders and its original President, in his first reference to her wrote in his private 'Journal' or diary, on 31st July 1888, of a curious incident connected with Miss Freer, whom he described as 'a friend of Fred Myers'. Apparently F. W. H. Myers or Miss Freer (or both) had told Sidgwick, some five weeks after the event, that on Sunday, 24th June 1888, the day after Gurney had been

---

[1] Myers became Joint Hon. Secretary of the S.P.R. after Gurney's death, and it seems inevitable that the policy of the Society would be influenced by his pronounced sympathy with the claims of spiritualism. This attitude of Myers, and the published opinions of him by contemporaries such as Lady Constance Battersea, Lady Caroline Jebb, and Sir Joseph Thompson, is discussed on pp. 37–48 of my *The Strange Case of Edmund Gurney*. It is plain from the unpublished correspondence between Lord Bute, a Vice-President of the S.P.R., and the Rev. Peter Dewar, that as late as 1894 it was regarded as regrettable that Myers was still attracted to 'the camp of spiritualism' and to patently fraudulent mediums.

[2] The Hornby imbroglio is described on pp. 65–8 of my book on Edmund Gurney.

found dead behind the locked door of a Brighton hotel bedroom, Miss Freer had a spontaneous and vivid supernormal conviction that some calamity had happened connected with her friend Myers, who was of course a close colleague of Gurney. Sidgwick was evidently much impressed by this example of Miss Freer's claim to clairvoyant ability, for he wrote that she had already experienced a number of similar telepathic impressions, and added of the Myers incident, 'What can this mean?' He had apparently no doubts about Miss Freer's truthfulness and sincerity, for he added, 'We think her a perfectly trustworthy witness.' When Eleanor and Arthur Sidgwick, Sidgwick's widow and brother, who were both prominent S.P.R. members, published the 'Journal' in *Henry Sidgwick, A Memoir* (London, 1906) they chose to omit the entire entry for 31st July 1888, which described both this incident and Sidgwick's views on the strange circumstances of Gurney's death. A few weeks later, in his 'Journal' of 10th September 1888, Sidgwick underlined his approval of Miss Freer. 'She is bright and clever and by no means credulous: altogether my impression of the evidential value of her remarkable series of experiences is raised.' As in the case of the earlier comment by Sidgwick, his biographers, in transcribing this entry in 1906, chose to suppress both Miss Freer's identity and Sidgwick's praise of her qualities, which it is difficult not to connect with other evidence, both published and unpublished, which suggests that the S.P.R. leaders may have revised their opinion of Miss Freer somewhat drastically in later years. It was not possible, however, to extinguish in 1906 approving comments by Sidgwick that had already been published. In 1894, for example, after taking the chair at a meeting of the S.P.R. at Westminster Town Hall on 8th June, at which Miss Freer read a paper, 'The Apparent Sources of Supernormal Experiences', Sidgwick praised the lecturer warmly indeed:

The Chairman, in expressing the thanks of the meeting to Miss X., remarked that it was rare to find the capacity for supernormal perception combined with the power of self-observation and analysis, the carefulness and promptitude in recording experiences, and the appreciation of the importance of different kinds of evidence, which Miss X's paper showed.[1]

---

[1] *Journal*, S.P.R., June 1894, p. 261. W. T. Stead proudly quoted Sidgwick in full, adding, 'A compliment from Professor Sidgwick is a compliment indeed, and those who read the "Notes" in our present issue will see how thoroughly it was deserved by my able and gifted assistant' (*Borderland*, July 1894, vol. I, p. 400).

The date and circumstances of the first meeting between Miss Freer and F. W. H. Myers are not known to me, but there can be little doubt that he admired her and that he was on much more intimate terms with her than were any of his colleagues. He seems to have introduced her to psychical research and the Society, to whose members he personally read her first two anonymous papers, 'Recent Experiments in Crystal-Vision' on 10th May 1889[1] and 'A Record of Telepathic and Other Experiences' on 25th October of the same year.[2] He was mainly responsible for her appointment as a paid assistant to W. T. Stead, the owner and editor of the spiritualist journal *Borderland*, and for other favours. We know from unpublished correspondence that it was through Myers that she was introduced in 1894 to Lord Bute, a Vice-President of the S.P.R. who became Miss Freer's generous patron. I have not been given access to Myers' papers, but Mr R. D. Stein, who presumably has, claims that according to a note by Myers, the couple first met in January 1888, when Myers wrote privately of Miss Freer's beautiful grey eyes, and said that she was in her middle twenties.[3] I cannot test the worth of this statement, for Mr Stein's article lacks any documentation, contains some errors of fact, and is completely wrong on one main point which is very relevant to any speculation regarding the relationship between Myers and Ada Freer. We are more likely to suspect a man who had indulged in a three-year liaison with his own cousin's wife, of seeking further sexual adventures than one who had not. The matter which Mr Stein has elected to raise in this connexion is an exchange of letters between Mr W. H. Salter, Dr A. Gauld of the S.P.R., and myself. It is fortunate that I have preserved this correspondence.

Mrs Marshall, the wife of Myers' first cousin and the mother of five young children, drowned herself in Ullswater in 1876, after trying to cut her throat with scissors, following a three-year passionate love-affair with Myers. Mr Stein mistakenly asserts that Mr Salter, one of the earliest S.P.R. members still living,[4] a Past President, and the Society's Honorary Secretary for over twenty years,

[1] *Proceedings*, S.P.R., 1888–9, vol. V, pp. 486–521.

[2] *Ibid.*, 1889–90, vol. VI, pp. 358–97.

[3] R. D. Stein, 'In Defence of F. W. H. Myers', *Fate*, Douglas, I.O.M., September 1965, pp. 47–61. This essay was, in essence, a violent criticism of Mr A. S. Jarman's recent study of the effect of Myers' relationship with Mrs A. E. Marshall, upon his attitude towards psychical research and the proof of survival, 'Failure of a Quest', *Tomorrow*, vol. 12, No. 1, pp. 17–29, and *Dr Gauld and Mr Myers*, London, 1964. Mr Stein's paper was marred by some mistakes, and Mr Jarman's reply (*Fate*, January 1966, pp. 26 ff.) makes entertaining reading.

[4] W. H. Salter has died since *Strange Things* was published.

and Dr A. Gauld, Myers' biographer, with the Myers papers at their disposal, wrote to me to ask if I had 'gleaned any information on Annie's pregnancy' in connexion with the tragedy. The exact reverse of this unlikely if flattering picture of myself as a fountain of knowledge is true. The facts are that I first read of Mrs Marshall's death, without any details or mention of suicide, in Mr Salter's 'F. W. H. Myers' Posthumous Message' (*Proceedings*, S.P.R., vol. LII, pp. 1–32). After seeing the death certificate and the inquest reports, I wrote spontaneously to Mr Salter, who in his reply openly spoke of Mrs Marshall's pregnancy at the time of her death as an established fact. This again was completely new information to me. When I later wrote to Dr Gauld, he told me that the secret had been passed to Mr Salter by S.P.R. leaders of the last generation, including Mrs E. M. Sidgwick, Sir Lawrence Jones, and Mr J. G. Piddington.

Whether Miss Freer was ever more than what Sidgwick called 'a friend of Fred Myers', we may never know with certainty. That Myers was a confessed sensualist and womanizer before his marriage to Eveleen Tennant in 1880 is not in dispute,[1] but it is fair to point out that many a 'lecher' (as Dr Gauld once described Myers to me) becomes a model husband. On the other hand, we must remember that Professor C. D. Broad has told us that Eveleen Myers was 'a singularly egotistical and rather unscrupulous person' and that Myers had marital difficulties.[2]

Any affair with Miss Freer would involve an assumption of Myers' infidelity to his marriage vows. In this connexion it is of interest to see that Mr Stein believes that Myers' love poem 'A Sister of Phyllis', which was included in his *Fragments of Inner Life*, privately circulated in a few copies after his death, was written about his brief association with a young widowed medium, Mrs Constance Julia Turner, in April 1890, when Myers had been married for ten years. Dr A. Gauld shares this view,[3] which has been put forward in opposition to the suggestion of Mr A. S. Jarman that the poem concerned Myers' earlier affair with Mrs A. E. Marshall.

'A Sister of Phyllis' contains expressions of Myers' admiration for the slenderness and fairness of the young woman concerned (whoever she was) and of 'The blue, the gold, of eyes, of hair', and the following lines, to which Mr Jarman has attached significance:

> *I spake; she listened; woman-wise*
> *Her self-surrendering answer came.*

[1] See, for example, the comments of Miss Helen Gurney and Lady Caroline Jebb, quoted on pp. 33, 38, 39, etc., of *The Strange Case of Edmund Gurney*.

[2] *Swan On a Black Sea*, edited by Signe Toksvig, with a Foreword by C. D. Broad, London, 1965, p. xix.   [3] *Journal*, S.P.R., June 1964, pp. 319–20.

It is fair to point out that Dr Gauld, while conceding that Myers 'several times went out by the sea alone with Constance, and he took her out again on 1st June [1890] when he was passing through Folkestone', nevertheless insists that there is no evidence 'for supposing that Myers was physically involved with Constance', or that the lines about her 'self-surrendering answer' necessarily refer to her seduction by Myers.[1] Dr Gauld may be right in these assumptions. On the other hand, if, as he thinks, the poem quoted does refer to Myers' association with Mrs Turner, then it is not easy to believe that there was not at least an emotional relationship between them.

In later years Miss Freer quarrelled bitterly with Myers, and in her published criticism of him, to be discussed later, the emotional overtones were fairly obvious. Despite her attractions, she did not marry until she was forty-eight, four years after Myers died, and at the time of his final illness and death she suffered a severe nervous and physical breakdown. Clearly, I think, there was a special relationship of some sort between the two, but how deeply it went is a matter for the judgment of the reader when he has considered the evidence. In this connexion the very odd business of Miss Freer's violent reaction to Myers taking Miss Chaston, a woman seven years younger than Miss Freer, to Ballechin House in 1897, and the diligent curiosity of Sir James Crichton-Browne and Lord Bute to find out who and what Miss Chaston really was, to be discussed later, is very relevant. Whatever the truth of the matter may

[1] *Journal*, S.P.R., June 1964, pp. 319–20. On the subject of Mr Stein's errors of fact, in his essay, it may be pointed out that his observation that the death of Constance Turner took place at Folkestone (p. 57) is quite wrong. Mrs Turner died on 10th August 1890, a few months after her meetings with Myers, at Abbey Lands, Weston-on-Trent, in the Midlands, her death being reported by her sister and fellow medium, Mrs Everett, of the same address. And as regards the accuracy of Dr Alan Gauld, the editor of the S.P.R. *Journal*, in his criticism of Mr Jarman, it may be pointed out that his explanation of why Mrs Marshall's body was taken for burial by her father to her old home at Thornton-le-Dale in Yorkshire, and not interred in Cumberland where her married life had been spent, was wholly wrong. Dr Gauld said (*Journal*, S.P.R., June 1964, p. 322) that 'prior to the Burial Laws Amendment Act of 1880, the burial of suicides presented difficulties, which Mr Hill could have overcome by burying his daughter in the parish of which he was himself rector'. Dr Gauld overlooked the fact that the verdict at the inquest contained the saving clause 'being of unsound mind' in regard to Mrs Marshall's suicide, which removed all burial difficulties, and he was evidently unaware, through failure to consult *Crockford*, that at the date of the tragedy Mr Hill had not been the rector of Thornton-le-Dale for nearly twenty years. The point is not lacking in importance. Dr Gauld was trying to counter Mr Jarman's argument that the removal of Mrs Marshall's body to distant Yorkshire by her father confirmed the very reasonable belief, for which there was other evidence, that Mrs Marshall and her husband became estranged during her affair with Myers.

be, the observation by Mr Stein that Myers and Miss Freer first met in 1888 does appear to be at variance with what seem to be the rather strong indications that they were in close contact with each other some years earlier. Clearly, anything Miss Freer wrote requires corroboration, but it is relevant to point out that she published a number of statements on this question during Myers' lifetime, which he could have contradicted if he had thought it appropriate to do so.

Miss Freer's work, albeit anonymously, first achieved prominence in psychical research circles by her unsigned paper on crystal-gazing, read to the Society for her by Myers in the Spring of 1889, and printed in full in the *Proceedings*. It was, she recorded, Myers who first put a crystal ball into her hands, asking her whether she had ever before experimented with anything of the kind. According to her, pictures soon presented themselves, and Myers allowed her to keep the 'treasured crystal', and for more than a year she experimented and gave the subject her most serious attention. She undertook, she said, a prolonged scholarly study of the history of the whole subject in the British Museum and elsewhere, and an investigation of all the literature, both ancient and modern, that she could find which touched upon crystal-gazing. This work, she recorded, was done as early as 1887, a statement which, if true, would in itself dispose of the suggestion that she and Myers first met in 1888.[1]

Some confirmation is available of this dating of her interest in crystal-gazing, in that before Myers introduced Miss Freer to this subject they had already done work together in automatic writing, in which Myers was keenly interested. She wrote during Myers' lifetime that her first experiments in this subject were undertaken 'in 1885 or 1886' at his urgent published plea.[2] This 'earnest appeal', as Myers called it, was printed by him at the end of a long paper on automatic writing dated 30th January 1885. He asked for first-hand testimony from spiritualists in England and America who were automatists, to be sent to him at the S.P.R. in London or to his home address.[3] He said that an earlier appeal in spiritualist papers had produced only meagre results. It seems more probable, on the face of it, that Miss Freer's response to this invitation would be 'in 1885 or 1886' rather than as late as 1888. If this first contact was indeed in, say, 1886, and was followed by the year's work on crystal-gazing in 1887, then the sequence of events would fit together very well, as will be seen.

[1] *Borderland*, 1895, vol. II, p. 263.   [2] *Ibid.*, 1896, vol. III, p. 169.
[3] F. W. H. Myers, 'Automatic Writing', *Proceedings*, S.P.R., 1885, vol. III, pp. 1–63.

In this connexion it is important to bear in mind that although the paper on crystal-gazing was not read to the Society and printed in its *Proceedings* until the Spring of 1889, it was in fact submitted to the S.P.R. in 1888, as Sidgwick said in his Foreword to the later paper on telepathy, also written by Miss Freer and read to the S.P.R. by Myers on 25th October 1889.[1] This was to be expected, when it is recalled that Miss Freer was a newcomer to the Society and that this was her first published work, however highly it may have been recommended by Myers. Sidgwick was obviously referring to the long and intricate first section of the crystal-gazing paper dealing with the history of the subject, which had required many months of literary study, in that the final section, presumably added as an afterthought at Myers' suggestion, consisted of some examples of Miss Freer's experiences stated to be copied from her notebooks, some of which ran into early 1889.

In the light of the foregoing it seems to me that Miss Freer's timetable of these events is more probable than the suggestion that she first met Myers in 1888, for an impossibly tight schedule would be involved if we try to fit the automatic writing, the crystal-gazing experiments, and the writing of the paper on that subject into that one year. Of this latter work she wrote:

When, in 1887, I devoted a considerable amount of leisure to investigating the subject [of crystal-gazing], I was mainly indebted for material, in what was then a somewhat remote research, to my acquaintance with folk-lore, and to those authors, classical and mediaeval, upon whom the writers on folk-lore mainly depend. It was necessary, not only to search the annals of Greece and Rome, of civilised Asia, of Egypt, and of mediaeval Europe, but to examine scores of pamphlets and rare tracts in various languages (as well as, of course, the recognised authorities) dealing with the peasant tales of Scandinavia and Russia, with legends and myths of American Indians and Pacific Islanders, with the tribes of Australia and New Zealand, and Southern Africa.[2]

These were large claims; but it can be said that her paper on this subject, immense in its length, was impressive in its obvious

---

[1] In this paper, prepared after the one on crystal-gazing, Miss Freer wrote (and Myers read out to the S.P.R.) that she was writing up some of her telepathic experiences for him as early as January 1888, which in itself makes it additionally difficult to believe that they first met in that year (*Proceedings, S.P.R.*, 1889-90, vol. VI, p. 370).

[2] *Borderland*, 1895, vol. II, p. 263. And it was Myers, according to her, who first introduced her to the subject by placing a crystal ball into her hands, an event which must have taken place some time before she began her investigations.

diligence and presentation of her material. It covered thirty-six closely printed pages of the S.P.R. *Proceedings*, and contained no less than eighty footnotes and references. She quoted many writers, both ancient and modern, famous and obscure, in her account of the history of the subject. If the work at the British Museum was done in 1887, and did take a year as she claimed, which might well have been, then this would bring the submission of the completed paper to the S.P.R. to 1888, as Sidgwick said. It is relevant also that Miss Freer stated that the greater part of the writing of the paper was done in the house of Myers' mother, which suggests in itself an earlier and a greater degree of familiarity with Myers than with the other S.P.R. leaders, as does the fact that in July 1888, some months after she had joined the Society, Sidgwick was still referring to her as 'a friend of Fred Myers', rather than as a member of the S.P.R.

The personal experiences in crystal vision and telepathy, told in Miss Freer's two papers on these subjects in 1889, were purely anecdotal. She had been able, she said, to obtain from the crystal the address, which she had inadvertently destroyed, of a person to whom she wished to write. As she had no other information, she wrote, she 'risked posting my letter to the address so strangely supplied'. The letter reached its destination.[1] She was successful in finding a missing medical prescription, which had been 'accidentally folded within one of E's letters, where it had remained, I have reason to believe, for more than four years'. The crystal provided the information as to its whereabouts.[2] A lost household key was similarly discovered after Miss Freer had 'applied to the crystal for information'.[3] Not a shred of evidence was offered regarding the location of these occurrences or the names of the persons involved. Indeed, when Miss Freer described how she was able to see in her crystal the details of the new decorations of a friend's house, her caution was such that not only did she conceal the name of the friend or where she lived but even the year in which the alleged incident took place.[4]

Miss Freer's second anonymous S.P.R. paper, this time dealing with her telepathic experiences, was even longer than her earlier contribution, occupying no less than forty pages of the *Proceedings*. As before, it was read to the Society by Myers, and Sidgwick provided a short Foreword. The style did not differ from that of the earlier paper. Her readers learned that Miss Freer had been enjoying psychical experiences 'extending over a life-time' from the age

---

[1] *Proceedings*, S.P.R., 1888–9, vol. V, p. 507.
[2] *Ibid.*, p. 509.　　　[3] *Ibid.*, p. 509.　　　[4] *Ibid.*, p. 512.

of three.[1] When she was fifteen she had been able telepathically to summon a friend who was eighty miles away. The friend arrived in a few hours.[2] As a child she had abandoned her 'favourite amusement of chess', she said, because her ability to foresee her opponents' intentions gave her such an advantage that her schoolboy friend had fallen into the reprehensible habit of betting on her invariable success.[3] She was able, by telepathy, to save the house of her friend 'D' from being burnt down.[4] As in the case of her crystal visions, Miss Freer refrained from giving either the names of the friends involved or the location of any of the incidents, so that neither criticism nor comment was, or is, possible. This was perhaps one of the reasons why these stories were so acceptable to the S.P.R. leaders, and why so many pages of the *Proceedings* were gratefully devoted to their publication. However this may be, there is no doubt that if this was the kind of material welcomed by the Society, then Miss Freer was willing to provide it in quantity at this period. This was additionally demonstrated by her contribution to Myers' series of immense papers on what he called 'The Subliminal Consciousness'.

The fifth of these papers was read by Myers to the Society at the Westminster Town Hall on 28th October 1892 and published in the *Proceedings*.[5] Many pages were written by Miss Freer, who by now was using her pseudonym of 'Miss X'. Myers, in introducing her contribution, said her phenomena were continuing steadily and increasing in value with each year of their continuance. They were also enlarging in scope, for as Myers revealed (p. 492), Miss Freer had now added the ability to receive psychical messages through seashells to her other talents. She herself explained this new gift and how she acquired it:

I have naturally exceedingly acute and sensitive hearing, which was developed by four years of scientific musical education, and it was with some hope that I possessed myself of a smooth-lipped cowrie of a size convenient to hold in the palm of the hand, applied it to my ear, and waited.[6]

[1] *Proceedings*, S.P.R., 1889–90, vol. VI, pp. 359–60. She commenced her paper with a general claim to supernormal ability, saying that throughout the whole of her life she had 'possessed some power of telepathic percipience, or susceptibility to the action of other minds, and at the same time some power of influencing them in a similar way'.
[2] *Ibid.*, p. 361.   [3] *Ibid.*, p. 361.   [4] *Ibid.*, pp. 367–8.
[5] F. W. H. Myers, 'The Subliminal Consciousness, V', *Proceedings*, S.P.R., 1892, vol. VIII, pp. 436–535. This section alone occupied a hundred pages of *Proceedings*. In the same volume two earlier sections had already been printed, covering over seventy pages.   [6] *Ibid.*, p. 493.

Results were rapidly forthcoming, and some of these were included in Myers' paper. He said on p. 492 that he hoped that Miss X's example as a successful shell-hearer would be followed by others interested in the subject. Only one of Miss Freer's anecdotes is worth repeating here, because of its connexion with George Albert Smith, Myers' private secretary. This young man, who in my opinion was indirectly responsible for Gurney's suicide, was later to be revealed as a ruthless trickster by his confederate Douglas Blackburn. At this time, however, Smith was contentedly receiving a salary from the S.P.R. leaders in exchange for deceiving them, before taking up once more his career as a showman in Brighton.[1] It is of some interest, therefore, to discover that Miss Freer and Smith were on friendly terms.[2]

According to Miss Freer's section of Myers' paper, Smith had visited her to engage in some successful thought-reading experiments. He left Miss Freer about seven p.m. After dinner Miss Freer took up her shell, which began to repeat some of Smith's engaging conversation earlier in the evening, in his voice, describing a walk over the rocks by the sea at Ramsgate in Kent. This was interrupted by the shell, still in Smith's voice, asking the curious and quite irrelevant question, 'Are you a vegetarian, then?' Miss Freer at once sat down and wrote a letter to Smith about this incident, to which Smith replied with equal promptitude. After leaving Miss Freer, he wrote, he had met an acquaintance whom he called 'Mr M',[3] who alluded in conversation to a vegetarian restaurant he knew, which caused Smith to ask the question Miss Freer heard in the shell. Smith said that the words quoted by Miss Freer were exactly those he had used, and there was no doubt 'that the shell spoke the truth'.[4] The only help I can offer to the reader in assessing the worth of this remarkable story is to remind him that Dr E. J. Dingwall has recently described the late George Albert Smith as 'an individual in whom well-informed persons today place only the slightest confidence'.[5] This opinion of Smith was held as early as

[1] The careers of Smith and Blackburn are described in my *The Strange Case of Edmund Gurney.*

[2] Professor J. O. Baylen has discovered among the papers of W. T. Stead a letter from F. W. H. Myers to Stead at this period, dated 5th December 1892, which refers to Miss Freer and Smith. Myers wrote, 'I thought that some of the cases which Miss Freer allowed me to see in MS. looked very good; and we will gladly help in working them up, if it prove possible. G. A. Smith, I think, has been instructed by Miss Freer on that point.'

[3] The identity of 'Mr M' was not revealed.

[4] *Proceedings*, S.P.R., 1892, vol. VIII, pp. 494–95.

[5] *Mediums of the 19th Century*, New York, 1963, vol. I, p. xv. This book is a reprint, with an introduction by Dr Dingwall, of Frank Podmore's *Modern*

1899, even before Douglas Blackburn's revelations were published. Mr R. P. Ellis, writing in *The Ethical World* on the early S.P.R. experiments in thought transference, observed:

The Creery children are exposed; and for some time now, it is well to remember, a Mr G. A. Smith is the link between Mrs Sidgwick, the usual controller of the experiments, and the indifferent class of individuals to whom he 'telepathically' transmits numbers and the like.

The percipients, the 'indifferent class of individuals', were a group of working-class youths in Brighton, friends of Smith, who were paid by the S.P.R. for the experiments, which depended entirely upon the integrity of Smith and the boys. Mr Ellis said of Smith:

Unknown as that gentleman is to the world, one may reasonably ask, on general grounds:

> *'Who is Smith? Ah! who is he,*
> *That all the world should trust him?'*

By 1892, as we shall see, Miss Freer had much to interest her besides the preparation of long papers for the S.P.R., however enthusiastic their reception may have been. To anticipate a little, however, it may be said that her last contribution to the *Proceedings* in any way comparable with her earlier efforts was printed in 1895, with the now customary introduction by Henry Sidgwick.[1] The paper was somewhat shorter than the previous ones, and was published over the pseudonym of 'Miss X', which Miss Freer had now been habitually using for two or three years.

One story in this paper is of some interest, as it possibly illustrates the methods used by Miss Freer in building up these psychical reminiscences. She was reading *Love's Labour Lost* [*sic*] in bed before rising, she wrote, when suddenly 'the picture I had conjured up disappeared, and gave place to the village street of my northern home'. Miss Freer added that the scene was out of date in that the rough stone cottages of her childhood days, in one of which an old family servant had lived, had now been displaced by a block of handsome stone buildings. She experienced an inexplicable sense of loss and distress, and tears sprang to her eyes. She knew that some

[1] 'On the Apparent Sources of Subliminal Messages', *Proceedings*, S.P.R., 1895, vol. XI, pp. 114–44.

Spiritualism, London, 1902. Dr Dingwall knew Smith, who lived to a great age. Attempts to put forward the contrary view against the weight of evidence available, notably by Mr Fraser Nicol, seem to have arisen from a lack of acquaintance with the literature.

tragedy had occurred. A moment later there was sad but complete confirmation of this 'subliminal message'. Miss Freer's maid entered the bedroom with the morning tea, together with a letter from a friend. The letter told Miss Freer that her 'dear old servant', the inhabitant of one of the cottages, a servant whom Miss Freer 'had known all my life, had died suddenly, and that my friends had just returned from the funeral service'.[1] It is almost superfluous to say that the reader was offered no clue of any kind as to the identity of the northern village, the dear old servant, or the sympathetic correspondent.

If this story had any ingredient of truth in it, then the scene with which Miss Freer had been familiar, the home of the servant she had known all her life, must have been in the town of Uppingham in the Midlands, where the first years of her life were spent, and not in a northern village at all. If, at any rate, we make this assumption, the result is not lacking in interest. The Freer family had lived in High Street in Uppingham until 1890, when Benjamin Freer, after living for a time at the White Hart, moved into nearby Orange Lane, which is now Orange Street. High Street is dominated by Uppingham School, which was much extended in the nineteenth century and may very appropriately be described as a 'block of handsome stone buildings'. If the reader is of the opinion that the superstructure of this engaging story was built up in this way, then the typical touches by Miss Freer regarding her reading of Shakespeare in bed before rising and the ministrations of her maid will not have escaped him.

[1] *Op. cit.*, pp. 138–9.

4

MISS FREER, *BORDERLAND*,
AND THE BURTON CASE

AS I have had occasion to say earlier, Miss Freer seems on the face of it to have enjoyed some degree of financial independence during the first years of her association with Myers. By the early 1890s, however, she had become interested in obtaining money from any source available to her. Certainly by September 1894, on the evidence of Sir William Huggins, she felt it necessary to borrow from Lord Bute, who was already paying through the S.P.R. for her Scottish tour.[1] She became employed in a minor and part-time administrative capacity from 1893 by the Swanley Horticultural College. In 1895 she moved as a permanent guest into the home of her friend Miss Constance Moore, daughter of the Rev. Daniel Moore, at Holy Trinity vicarage, Paddington, London, thereby presumably reducing her living expenses.[2] Most importantly she became, apparently from 1892 at latest, the paid assistant of W. T. Stead, who in the following year was to begin the publication of the spiritualist quarterly *Borderland*, of which Miss Freer became assistant editor.

William Thomas Stead (1849–1912), the radical journalist and author, editor of the *Pall Mall Gazette* and the *Review of Reviews*, had been introduced to the attractions of spiritualism in 1880 and

---

[1] On 2nd February 1895 she complained to Lord Bute of the difficulty in which she had been placed by the S.P.R.'s delay in paying some of her expenses, amounting to £45, from money provided by Bute, adding that she had no idea how the S.P.R. spent 'its large income and its frequent legacies and donations'. Whether this criticism had any foundation in fact, or whether it was merely a hint that a further loan from Bute would be agreeable, I do not know.

[2] Daniel Moore (1809–99) was the Vicar of Holy Trinity, Paddington, and Rural Dean of Paddington until 1895. He was Chaplain-Ordinary to Queen Victoria and Prebendary of St Paul's. He was the son of George Moore, a Coventry ribbon manufacturer, and his wife, Hannah Shaw, the daughter of another industrialist. When Miss Freer came to live in his house he was eighty-five. When the Moores removed to 27 Cleveland Gardens, Hyde Park, Miss Freer moved with them, remaining there until she and Miss Constance Moore set up house together at The Laurels, Bushey Heath, Hertfordshire.

had become an ardent believer.[1] He met Miss Freer in the autumn of 1891, and like most men who came into contact with her at this period, Stead was immediately captivated. He wrote of her to a friend:

I have just lunched with a young lady who has seen five of her relations and friends who have appeared to her at the moment of death. She has already seen an indefinite number of others, and sees in the crystal—in short, has a personal practical experience of almost every kind of phenomenal apparition, and is not in the least spoiled by it. She is, I think, about 25, and is devoted to good works; lives in Society, has had a first-class education, and is perfectly self-possessed.[2]

According to Miss Freer, it was through Myers that her first meeting with Stead was arranged. She wrote:

It must have been in the summer of 1891 that I first came into touch with my revered and valued friend W. T. Stead. I had recently contributed to the pages of the Proceedings of the Society for Psychical Research *a paper upon 'Some Experiments in Crystal Gazing'* [sic]. *This, in deference to prejudice on the part of my family had been strictly anonymous, and indeed the greater part of it was written not at home, but when upon a visit to Mrs Frederic Myers, the mother of Mr F. W. H. Myers, though it was the result of prolonged study at the British Museum and elsewhere.*

I received a letter from Mr Myers asking permission to reveal my identity to the well-known journalist, who had not been altogether in sympathy with the work of the Society, but who desired nevertheless to make my acquaintance. Mr Myers added that Mr Stead was engaged upon the work afterwards published as Real Ghost Stories, *and was therefore in communication with a great number of people who might be of use to psychical research, and to whom Mr Myers suggested I might be the means of 'bringing into line'.*

I wrote to Mr Stead that I hoped to call upon him when we returned

---

[1] Estelle Stead, *My Father, Personal and Spiritual Reminiscences*, London 1913, pp. 95–103. According to Miss Stead, it was Mr Mark Fooks who first introduced Stead to psychic matters. Stead attended his first séance in 1881, when he was told by the medium that he would become 'the St Paul of Spiritualism'. Although Miss Stead describes the founding and publication of *Borderland* in some detail, Miss Freer's name is mentioned nowhere in her book.

[2] *The Life of W. T. Stead*, vol. II, p. 38. Whyte said of Stead (*ibid.*, vol. I, p. 247) that he was always an easy prey for adventuresses. Of his acquaintance with Mrs Gordon-Baillie, 'the fair seductress', in the late 1880s, Stead's biographer wrote that had it been safe for this lady to stay in London, 'the consequences to Stead's private purse might have been serious indeed; he was always an easy prey even to less accomplished swindlers'.

*to London in the Autumn, and on 10th October I paid a visit to Mow-
bray House, Norfolk Street, which is memorable to me in many ways.
It was an adventure for a girl[1] brought up by an elderly relative with
early Victorian standards, to find herself in the presence of a non-
conformist journalist, in a London office; an adventure undertaken
secretly so far as my home was concerned, though with the knowledge
of the friends whom I was visiting, and who had sent with me a trusted
family servant . . .*

*He wished me to collaborate in the book he was writing, and to lunch
with him at Gatti's, in the Strand one day a week to discuss progress.
I was obliged to decline, but offered to contribute anonymously, to the
book, in which, as a matter of fact, there was eventually a good deal of
my work . . .*

*Within a few months changes occurred which freed me from the more
extreme of the conventional austerities he so much deprecated, although,
when in the following spring I agreed to become joint editor of an Occult
Journal, it was still necessary that I should be known only as 'Miss X',
and that arrangements should be made which should obviate the necessity for my frequenting Mowbray House, and taking my place as a
member of the staff. Rooms were taken in Pall Mall East, and a
married lady engaged as my secretary. I was to visit the office occasionally only, and to see no one except by appointment. Nothing could
have been kinder or more generous than the spirit in which Mr Stead
met this necessity of circumstance, a kindness all the more generous in
that he was wholly out of sympathy with the social restrictions in
question. In a certain sense they annoyed him; he was specially annoyed
that I declined to have my portrait published in* Borderland. *There was,
however, from the journalistic point of view a certain value in the
mystery in which the personality of 'Miss X' was enshrouded . . .*

It was the last number of the year [during the third year of Border-
land] *and my Chief signified his appreciation by sending me for a
Christmas present a deed of gift of all property in* Borderland, *to take
effect in the year 1900, 'by which time', he was kind enough to add, my
commercial education would be as complete as my literary experience.
I showed the document to the late Marquis of Bute, whose interest in
psychical research is well known, and he congratulated me heartily,
proposing himself as a partner, and saying, 'It shall be the biggest
thing of the kind in Europe.'[2]* Borderland, *however, did not live to*

[1] Miss Freer was thirty-four years old in October 1891.

[2] Professor J. O. Baylen says that Stead's papers do not mention this alleged
deed of gift. Miss Freer's 109 letters to Lord Bute, covering the period from their
first meeting in May 1894 to July 1899, shortly before Bute's first apoplectic
seizure in August of that year, are completely silent on the subject. Stead left
nothing to Miss Freer in his will.

47

1900 and the Marquis passed away during that year. During this same absence [Stead was abroad] Mr Stead asked me to take charge of certain of his private benefactions and to see to their administration. It was a further revelation of his wonderful charity and large-heartedness. They were a curious collection of people, these recipients of his bounty, and after careful study of the paper connected with their stories and antecedents, and some observation of the people themselves, I could not but feel that in some cases he was being badly imposed upon. He was deeply hurt when I suggested to him, on his return, that the liberal sums expended should be administered by the Charity Organisation Society.[1]

This tribute to Miss Freer's 'revered and valued friend W. T. Stead' was written after the death of both Stead and Lord Bute, both of whom had been Miss Freer's generous patrons and between whom there had been little sympathy. The unpublished correspondence between Miss Freer and Lord Bute, and between Lord Bute and the Rev. Peter Dewar, shows that Stead's kindness had aroused no loyalty in Miss Freer. As early as June 1894, when she saw the better opportunity offered by the patronage of Lord Bute, with whom she had established herself in the previous month, she found it convenient to deny emphatically that she was 'an adherent of Steadism'. On 2nd February 1895 she told Bute that 'The stuff that passes for Astrology in *Borderland* is beneath criticism', and on 2nd October of the same year she confided to her new patron that the embarrassment of her paid appointment with *Borderland* had become a matter of conscience with her as well as of taste. On 15th December 1895 she wrote, possibly hopefully and certainly rather oddly in view of her subsequent letters, that her agreement with Stead was not legally binding and that after 'a harried and hurried week' with Stead she had settled her affairs with him at 'considerable money loss' to herself.

In the event the prickings of conscience were evidently not effective, for she continued with her salaried work for Stead, while her criticisms of him to Lord Bute became more positive. On 6th January 1896, the year in which she afterwards said in print that Stead had been especially generous to her, she wrote to Bute that the next issue of *Borderland* would contain, to her regret, 'some dissenting profanities of Mr Stead's', but that for the sake of the public she was doing her best with the magazine. Later in the same month, on 25th January, she told Bute that Stead was publishing

[1] Quoted from a contribution by Miss Freer to E. K. Harper, *Stead: The Man*, London, 1918, pp. 63–8.

statements in *Borderland* that he knew to be false. On 30th March 1896 she wrote to Bute (possibly hopefully), 'My *Borderland* affairs, *i.e.* my relations with the magazine, are very disagreeable to me, but I cannot afford to break them as I should lose £200 a year'. One wonders, in parenthesis, what Lord Bute thought of this statement in the light of Miss Freer's letter to him of 9th July 1894, two months after their first meeting, when she had already been employed by Stead for three years. She wrote, 'I regard my time as wholly at the disposal of the Society for Psychical Research [with which Stead had no connexion] so long as I am existing, in great part, at the Society's expense owing to your Lordship's liberality.' And if the story of Stead's extreme generosity to her in 1896 (the third year of *Borderland*) had any truth in it, a letter from her published in the *Oban Times* on 17th October of that year, extolling the value of the S.P.R. Second Sight Enquiry and the liberality of Lord Bute, was singularly unkind to Stead. She wrote, 'My interest in the phenomena has absolutely nothing to do with journalism as represented by Mr W. T. Stead, or any other editor to whose periodicals I may at any time contribute.' This was untrue as well as ungenerous. She was the assistant editor of *Borderland* under her pseudonym of 'Miss X', and not merely a contributor to it. At this particular time, moreover, Stead was abroad and she was running the paper herself on his behalf. It may be added that after *Borderland* had ceased publication in 1897, and the embarrassment of her salary of £200 a year from Stead had been discontinued, Miss Freer's criticisms of him to Lord Bute did not abate. In a letter to Lord Bute of 9th May 1898, for example, she advised that friends of his with alleged mediumistic gifts should not be allowed to fall into the hands of Stead, who would merely exploit them.

With the knowledge of Miss Freer's private opinion of Stead at his disposal, the reader is in a position to follow the development of her association with the proprietor of *Borderland* from the date of their first meeting, as described by her, in the summer of 1891. By October and November 1891 Stead and Miss Freer were meeting continually in London, and Frederic Whyte, Stead's biographer, evidently had access to some of Stead's hurried notes to her at this time, although very oddly these letters and all other such papers connected with Miss Freer have since disappeared. There can be no doubt about Stead's admiration for her qualities and his belief in her alleged spiritualistic abilities. He wrote to her on 12th November 1891, 'I telepathed madly to you this morning to come at 12 o'clock.' On 16th December of the same year he wrote, 'I recognize with great satisfaction the methodical neatness with which you do your work, and I heartily wish that you could infuse a little bit of that eminent virtue into my veins.'[1]

The first number of *Borderland* appeared in July 1893. In his introductory article Stead described Miss Freer as 'my assistant editor, Miss X'. Myers was delighted, and Stead printed a letter from him in the same issue, saying that Myers observed with pleasure that the lady known in S.P.R. *Proceedings* as 'Miss X' had consented to aid Stead in his task.[2]

Dr Campbell once wrote to me that *Borderland* may be not unfairly described as a chronicle of the incredible, written by and for the credulous. Certainly the following statement by Stead about Miss Freer, published in the first issue, is of great interest to the student of the psychology of testimony:

However incredible it may appear, I can, and do constantly, receive messages from my assistant editor, Miss X, as accurately and as constantly as I receive telegrams from those with whom I do business, without the employment of any wires or any instrument. Whenever I wish to know where she is, whether she can keep an appointment, or how she is progressing with her work, I simply ask the question and my hand automatically writes out the answer.

There is no consciousness on her part that I have asked the question, and received her answer. Distance does not affect the messages, they are received equally when she is asleep or awake . . . How it is done I do not pretend to know. That it is done is certain. It is no longer an experiment, it is a practical, every-day addition to the conveniences of human intercourse.[3]

As might have been expected, this statement aroused much published scepticism. The magazine *Black and White,* in its issue of 22nd July 1893, suggested sarcastically that despite these miracles, in certain stagnant and unprogressive offices the sixpenny telegram might still be useful. The *Glasgow Herald* on 17th July 1893 said that it was very difficult to accept the story of the alleged powers of the remarkable assistant editor 'Miss X', adding, 'Mr Stead may, as we have said, be perfectly honest in this matter, but if he is, then so much the worse for Mr Stead'.

These and other criticisms did not prevent Stead persisting in his claim that there was complete and continuous *rapport* between Miss Freer and himself. He wrote in the same volume of *Borderland*:

[1] *The Life of W. T. Stead*, vol. II, p. 38.
[2] *Borderland*, 1893–4, vol. I, p. 15.   [3] *Ibid.*, p. 6.

When Miss X, my assistant editor on Borderland, *returned from her recent interesting expedition in search of the gifted seers of the Highlands, she wrote telepathically with my hand, a long report covering three closely written quarto pages, describing the result of her visits, her plans and intentions in the future, reporting upon the condition of the office and its work, and discussing questions of practical business. All this was written out with my hand at Wimbledon, while Miss X was in town. I had not seen her for nearly six weeks, during which time I had not once written to her. When I met her I read over to her her telepathic message. When I had finished, she said, 'You have made one mistake. You say, "So-and-so is very painstaking, but very stupid." That is not my opinion. So-and-so is very painstaking, but only occasionally stupid.' And that was the only error in three closely-written quarto pages!* [1]

Whyte quotes a story by Stead about his psychic lady friend, clearly Miss Freer, who had promised to lunch with him in London. Wishing to know definitely whether she would keep the appointment, he placed his pen on a piece of paper and mentally asked her the question. She replied telepathically, and Stead's hand wrote out a disturbing message. A man alone in a railway carriage with her had made improper advances to her:

I was alarmed and repelled him. He refused to go away and tried to kiss me. I was furious. We had a struggle. I seized his umbrella and struck him, but it broke and I was beginning to fear he would master me, when the train began to slow up before arriving at Guildford station. He got frightened, let go of me, and before the train reached the platform he jumped out and ran away. I was very much upset. [2]

Miss Freer's appointment as assistant editor of *Borderland* in 1893 was a milestone in her career. This was her opportunity to spread her wings, and she immediately became a substantial contributor of long articles, reviews, and editorials under her pseudonym of 'Miss X'. She was an able and a prolific writer and succeeded, for a time at least, in the difficult task of obtaining the best of both worlds in occult matters. She assumed, on the one hand, the respectability of a mild impartiality and agnosticism, while at the same time showing a kindly tolerance for the fantastic claims of the spiritualists and making the most of her own allegedly supernormal experiences. The reader may think, moreover, from the following advertisement, which appeared in the first volume of *Borderland* over the address of Miss Freer's very private office in Pall Mall, that although Stead

[1] *Op. cit.*, p. 50   [2] *The Life of W. T. Stead*, vol. I, p. 326.

undoubtedly paid her generously, she was not disinclined to make a little extra money privately if she could:

A Lady, with considerable psychical experience, not a Spiritualist, will be happy to advise, by correspondence, in the conduct of experiments in Thought-Transference, Crystal-Gazing, Automatic Writing, and other forms of Automatism. Terms on application. Letters addressed to 'Psychic', Borderland Office, 18 Pall Mall East, will be forwarded.[1]

In my view, further light is thrown on the financial relationship between Stead and Miss Freer at this period by an incident mentioned by Myers in one of his papers on 'The Subliminal Consciousness'. I do not think that there can be any doubt that the lady friend of Stead's upon whom Myers said he would 'bestow the name of Miss Summers' in 1893 was Miss Freer. She was, as we know, strictly preserving her anonymity at that time. Myers said that 'Miss Summers' was 'the most important of Stead's telepathic correspondents', and that Stead 'almost every day received communication' by automatic writing from his friend. 'Miss Summers,' wrote Myers, moreover, 'was engaged on literary work of a kind needing much care and accuracy.' The identification with Miss Freer can scarcely be doubted. This being so, it is of interest to discover from Myers that when in September 1893 'Miss Summers' was temporarily short of money, Stead generously assisted.[2]

The pages of *Borderland* reveal much of the strange personality of Miss Freer, and of the social and intellectual world in which she lived between 1893 and 1897, the years of the magazine's existence. In *Borderland*, too, can be found much more detailed reports of her visits to the Highlands and the Islands of Scotland in connexion with the Second Sight Enquiry by the S.P.R. than appeared in the *Journal* of that organization. These journeys, in which she was usually accompanied by her ever-faithful friend Miss Constance Moore, have been discussed in *Strange Things*. Their importance from my point of view is that they establish the fact that by 1894 Miss Freer had contrived to secure for herself another wealthy patron, Lord Bute, who paid for these expeditions. It will be convenient, however, to include a general comment upon the relationship between Miss Freer and this wealthy and distinguished if eccentric Vice-President of the S.P.R. in a later discussion of the controversial Clandon affair.

A case of which *Borderland* and the S.P.R. made much was that of the 'Burton Messages', in which Miss Freer was the medium in a

---

[1] *Borderland*, 1893–4, vol. I, p. 383.
[2] *Proceedings*, S.P.R., 1893–4, vol. IX, pp. 52–4.

series of séances in July and August 1895, and produced by means of alleged automatic writing a number of messages supposed to emanate from the spirit of Lady Burton's husband, Sir Richard Francis Burton, the famous explorer and scholar who had died on 20th October 1890. After the first of these experiences Miss Freer wrote to Lord Bute to say that it 'has left me quite prostrate, and I am only just beginning to feel capable of travel'. On 26th August she wrote:

Lady Burton is deeply impressed by the characteristic language and the curious details, and has already altered her will on the strength of certain statements of which I hardly understand the import. As one issue is that she has left me Sir Richard's valuable Arabian and Egyptian occult instruments (crystal, magic mirror, etc.) I can't complain.

After Lady Burton's death on 22nd March 1896 Miss Freer published two accounts of the affair in *Borderland* in April 1896 [1] and January 1897.[2] In view of the theme and contents of these stories it is odd that concurrently with the publication of the first she wrote to Lord Bute on 2nd April 1896, saying:

The S.P.R. folk are greatly excited over the Burton business and want me to speak upon it on April 24th, which postpones my departure for Scotland till the 27th or 28th. Mr Myers is more convinced of the identity of Sir R. Burton than am I. I don't feel that Lady B. was as good a witness as I could wish.

Miss Freer also read a paper on the Burton case, 'Some Recent Experiences, Apparently Supernormal', to the 83rd General Meeting of the Society for Psychical Research at the Westminster Town Hall on 4th December 1896, with the President, William Crookes, in the chair. The address was received with enthusiasm, and at the end of Miss Freer's paper Crookes said 'that he had never heard a paper more scientifically thought out or more clearly expressed'.[3]

---

[1] 'Some Thoughts on Automatism. With the Story of the Burton Messages. By Miss X', *Borderland*, 1896, vol. III, pp. 157-72.

[2] 'More About the Burton Messages. By Miss X', *ibid.*, 1897, vol. IV, pp. 37-42. W. T. Stead commented with warm approval upon Miss Freer's paper, and it would seem that there was really no limit to his belief in her stories. He wrote, 'Miss X contributes some light upon the famous communications from Sir Richard Burton—communications which, it is curious to know, have excited the liveliest interest in the Vatican, and have led to friendly messages from His Holiness the Pope to Miss X' (*Review of Reviews*, January 1897, p. 56). As the Vatican was on the point of issuing its first condemnation of attempts to communicate with the dead, such a tale seems completely incredible.

[3] *Ibid.*, p. 42, and *Journal*, S.P.R., January 1897, p. 7.

The address was reported at some length in the Society's *Journal*,[1] but the warm approval of the S.P.R. and its President was not supported by the legitimate Press. Sharp criticisms were published, particularly in *St James's Gazette*, the *Westminster Gazette*, and the *World*, this last describing the meeting as a 'peculiarly nauseating recrudescence of offensive spiritualistic balderdash', and Miss Freer's account of the séances as 'vulgar imposture'.

We cannot now determine the precise truth of the matter, for the most important witness, Lady Burton, had died a month before Miss Freer published her first account, and could neither contradict nor confirm its contents. Miss Freer asserted (the reader may think typically) that her story could be corroborated by her friend, 'the Hon. Mrs G., now abroad', but nothing more seems to have been heard about this lady. According to Miss Freer, the first messages from Sir Richard Burton were received on her ouija board on 25th July 1895 when she was 'staying at their country house with Mr & Mrs D'.[2] Who Mr and Mrs D. were, and where their country house was located, Miss Freer did not reveal. Lady Burton was not, of course, present and knew nothing of these sittings. According to Miss Freer's account, the communicating spirit instructed the sitters to inform Lady Burton that messages from her late husband were being received. Miss Freer said that after discussion between her friends and herself it was decided to send a copy of the notes of the sittings to Lady Burton as a matter of duty.

The result could have been foreseen. Miss Freer was invited to Lady Burton's home at Mortlake on 5th August 1895. Sittings were given by Miss Freer with the aid of her ouija board, and Sir Richard obligingly communicated directly with his widow. The rather uninspiring messages did not differ in style from those usually associated with spiritualistic séances. As a variation, Miss Freer changed to crystal-gazing, and described the visions she saw to Lady Burton.

These events were interrupted by Miss Freer's second Scottish tour in the late summer of 1895, and she and Lady Burton never met again. As has been said, within a few weeks of Lady Burton's death in March 1896 Miss Freer published the whole story in *Borderland*, to be followed by her address to the S.P.R. There was, however, another and very different version of the affair, which was to be published a year later.

William Henry Wilkins (1860–1905), of Clare College, Cambridge, as the *Dictionary of National Biography* records, 'came to know intimately the widow of Sir Richard Burton and after her death

[1] 'General Meeting', *Journal*, S.P.R., January 1897, pp. 3–7.
[2] *Borderland*, 1896, vol. III, p. 163.

wrote *The Romance of Isabel, Lady Burton* (1897), a sympathetic memoir founded mainly upon Lady Burton's letters and autobiography.'[1] It is indicative of the friendship and good faith existing between Lady Burton and Wilkins that it was on her directions given during her lifetime that he edited in 1898 a revised edition of Lady Burton's own biography of her husband, *The Life of Sir Richard Burton*, and her *The Passion Play at Ober-Ammergau* (1900), as well as Sir Richard Burton's unpublished *The Jew, the Gypsy, and El Islam* (1898) and *Wanderings in Three Continents* (1901).

Wilkins's book on Lady Burton was dedicated to her sister, Mrs Gerald Fitzgerald, who was involved in his account of the affair of the messages. He first quoted from a letter written by Lady Burton to her friend Mrs Francis Joly on 17th April 1890, in which the former lady's attitude to spiritualism was made extremely clear. Lady Burton regarded the subject as 'a decoy to a crowd of sensation-seekers, who yearn to see a ghost as they would go to see a pantomime', and said that spiritualism, 'when not absolutely farcical, worked for evil, and not for good'. She advised Mrs Joly never to practise or interest herself in such matters, but to debar them from her house. She said, 'There is a spiritualism (I hate the word!) that comes from God, but it does not come in this guise. This sort is from the spirits of evil.' It says much for Miss Freer's ingratiating personality that while holding those views, Lady Burton was nevertheless caught in the toils for a brief period.

Wilkins wrote:

I have dwelt on this side of Lady Burton's character in order to contradict many foolish rumours. During the last years of her life in England, when her health was failing, she was induced against her better judgment to have some dealings with certain so-called 'spiritualists', who approached her under the plea of 'communicating' with her husband, thus appealing to her at the least point of resistance. Lady Burton told her sister that she wanted to see 'if there was anything in it', and to compare it with the occultism of the East. In the course of her inquiries she unfortunately signed certain papers which contained ridiculous 'revelations'. On thinking the matter over subsequently, the absurdity of the thing struck her. She came to the conclusion that there was nothing in it at all, and that, as compared with the occultism of the East, this was mere kindergarten. *She then wished to recall the papers. She was very ill at the time, and unable to write herself; but she mentioned the matter to her sister at Eastbourne, a short time before her death, and said, 'The first thing I do when I get back to London will be*

[1] *Dictionary of National Biography, Second Supplement*, 1912, vol. III, p. 667.

to recall those silly papers.' She was most anxious to return to London for this purpose; but the day after her return she died. Mrs Fitzgerald at once communicated Lady Burton's dying wishes to the person in whose charge the papers were, and requested that they should not be published. But with a disregard alike for the wishes of the dead and the feelings of the living, the person rushed some of these absurd 'communications' into print within a few weeks of Lady Burton's death, and despite all remonstrance was later proceeding to publish others, when stopped by a threat of legal proceedings from the executors.[1]

If this version of the story by Wilkins was the true one, and the messages allegedly from Sir Richard Burton were fraudulently produced by Miss Freer to deceive his widow, it can fairly be said that the imposture was a peculiarly cruel and heartless one. If there was a motive, it was presumably a financial one. Wilkins wrote, six pages before his account of the business of the séances, of Lady Burton's extreme and foolish generosity with money. Such was her enthusiasm for giving to beggars in the street, her biographer wrote, that she frequently returned home with an empty purse. Lady Burton's attitude in the face of criticism of this indiscriminate almsgiving was that she would rather give to ten rogues than turn one honest man away.[2]

The indications are, I fancy, that what Wilkins said was probably accurate. His account was corroborated by Lady Burton's sister. He was right in regard to Lady Burton's failing health, for in her first paper in *Borderland*, before any criticisms were made, Miss Freer revealed that Lady Burton 'had been for some years in a critical state of health',[3] and therefore, the reader may think, especially vulnerable to an approach by Miss Freer on the subject of her husband, her 'least point of resistance', as Wilkins called it. If we seek an explanation for the willingness of Lady Burton, an avowed opponent of spiritualism, to listen to Miss Freer in 1895, we may think that Miss Freer herself supplied the answer when she said that Lady Burton 'had suffered so severely from a sense of giddiness and brain confusion, that she had been to see a specialist'.[4] There is no doubt at all, moreover, that Wilkins was right in saying that Miss Freer rushed the Burton story into print with indecent

---

[1] W. H. Wilkins, *The Romance of Isabel, Lady Burton*, London, 1897, vol. II, pp. 767–8.

[2] *Ibid.*, p. 761. Another possible motive is suggested by the advice of the spirit of Sir Richard Burton to his widow, through Miss Freer's mediumship, that Lady Burton should employ forthwith a 'capable literary secretary' who was not to be a 'mere typewriting clerk'. *Borderland*, 1896, vol. III, p. 166.

[3] *Borderland*, 1896, vol. III, p. 168.   [4] *Ibid.*, p. 167.

haste within a week or two of Lady Burton's death in March 1896, for the first paper was published in *Borderland* in April. It seems pretty obvious, too, that something very drastic occurred to prevent Miss Freer giving further promised publicity to the case, and the threat of legal proceedings described by Wilkins seems a likely explanation. There is no doubt that Miss Freer, encouraged by the enthusiastic reception of her address to the S.P.R.,[1] *did* intend to publish a paper on the Burton case in the *Proceedings*. She wrote in her second essay in *Borderland* in January 1897, when she was answering the Press criticisms of her address in the previous month, that it was her intention to offer proof of her statements. She wrote, 'That proof will, indeed, be forthcoming in the article that I am about to contribute to the *Proceedings of the Society for Psychical Research*.'[2] It never was, for she was henceforward completely silent on the subject of the Burton messages. Despite Crookes's praise of Miss Freer, the S.P.R. published nothing more. The name of Burton was never mentioned again in *Borderland*, and Miss Freer refrained from any comment on the case in her book, *Essays in Psychical Research*, published in 1899.

The Burton case was probably Miss Freer's first mistake, and it may well be that she realized it. It was not to be the last, however, as the reader will learn. Despite the advantages of her friendship with Lord Bute, her increasing arrogance, coupled with her reckless self-confidence and lack of scruple, was to lead her into a series of difficulties, culminating in the final disaster that overtook her in 1901.

[1] F. W. H. Myers was personally enthusiastic. In an unpublished letter to Lord Bute on 3rd April 1896 he said that the case was 'a very good one' and that he wanted Miss Freer to visit the Burton mausoleum.

[2] *Borderland*, 1897, vol. IV, p. 39.

5

MISS FREER, LORD BUTE, AND THE CLANDON AFFAIR

JOHN PATRICK CRICHTON-STUART (1847–1900), third Marquess of Bute, was the immensely wealthy owner of estates in Scotland and Wales, and the munificent benefactor of both Glasgow and St Andrews Universities, being Rector of the latter ancient and beautiful seat of learning in 1892 and in 1898. His friend F. W. H. Myers described him as 'a great chieftain, a great magnate, a great proprietor, yet withal a figure, a character, which carried one back into the Ages of Faith'.[1] Myers added:

The youth whose vast wealth and eager religion suggested (it was said) to Lord Beaconsfield the idea of his Lothair *had become constantly wealthier and more religious as years went on. Amid the palaces of his structure and of his inheritance, he lived a life simple and almost solitary; a life of long walks and long conversations on the mysteries of the world unseen.*[2]

I have copies of some ninety-five letters written by Myers to Bute from 1890, shortly after Bute had joined the S.P.R., to the end of the Ballechin affair, when coolness developed between the two, exemplified in Bute's last letter to Myers in which he said that *The Alleged Haunting of B—— House* was 'self-defence against imputations publicly made by yourself and others' and that the book 'constitutes an implicit argument against your conclusions'. Myers' letters were, however, ingratiating in tone and contents, and Myers' flattery was often so exuberant that one wonders whether it was not an embarrassment to Lord Bute. Bute was, in Myers' view, an outstanding man of business, yet his nature was unusually kind and generous and his life entirely beneficient and universally valued. He was an outstanding example of thoroughness in all he did, wrote Myers, being gifted with noble perseverance. Bute's letters constituted a wealth of learning. He was a great archaeologist and historian, and he was the one man in the world, Myers considered, who could pronounce upon the relationship between the Catholic faith and psychical research. He was, according to Myers, the only conceivably possible

[1] *Journal*, S.P.R., November 1900, p. 310.   [2] *Ibid.*, p. 311.

Rector of St Andrews University. The 'majestic pile' at Mount Stuart, which Bute built and which Myers said he intensely admired, told of a combination of noble qualities in Bute that went far beyond mere wealth and lineage. A photograph of Bute's profile, wrote Myers, was *magnificent* (Myers' underlining), and suggested to Myers a majestic idea of one of the Early Fathers of the Universal Church. And yet, with all these superhuman qualities, Bute could be an exquisite humorist when he chose. His anecdotes, wrote Myers, were intensely funny.

Myers' acquiescence in all Bute said was constant throughout the correspondence. The whole of the opinions of the noble lord were of the utmost value and interest, and had Myers' immediate and unqualified agreement. 'I bow to what you say re Hinton-Ampner [a haunted house],' wrote Myers in February 1893. Bute had *forgotten* more than one unfortunate dissentient *knew*, in Myers' underlined opinion. Myers joined with Bute in wondering how Andrew Lang, who also became Rector of St Andrews and a President of the S.P.R., could write such 'superficial stuff'. If Bute thought there might be something in spirit photography, then so did Myers. On the other hand, although Myers had incautiously told Bute that he had been trying to persuade Miss Florence Marryat, a prolific writer of mediocre fiction and an enthusiastic spiritualist and amateur medium, to give some sittings for the S.P.R., he later obligingly confessed that he did not regard any statement by her 'as worth a moment's consideration'. This obsequiousness was at times faintly ridiculous. To quote one example, Bute took Myers mildly to task for using what he called 'feeble envelopes' for his correspondence; obviously one had burst open in the post. Myers wrote, 'Thank you! I take to heart your warning re feeble envelopes and will remember it to my dying day.'

The object of all this was made pretty clear by the correspondence. Myers was anxious to bring Bute into closer relationship with the S.P.R. and to persuade him to make substantial financial contributions to its work, especially that in which Miss Freer was involved. Bute was made a Vice-President of the Society shortly after becoming a member, and Myers wrote to ask if he would care to join the Council, and become a member of the Literary Committee. Bute wisely refused these two additional distinctions, on the grounds that he was too busy. But the first 'extremely munificent gift' was forthcoming by December 1892, which was later devoted to the Second Sight Enquiry in Scotland. In 1894 'further generosity' was acknowledged, with the encouraging comment by Myers that his mother had left no less than £3,000 to the S.P.R. Myers added that two wealthy members, Lady Caithness and the Duc de Pomar, had made wills 'leaving for a cognate purpose their large possessions'. 'But *that* is very risky,' wrote Myers, 'as the Duc de Pomar is only about forty, and may marry and upset it all any day. Meantime, we rub along with some difficulty and are grateful for whatever adds respectability to our bankers' account.' The implication was clear; the money would be welcome now.[1] Indeed, on 30th July 1896 Myers told Bute that Miss Freer was going to the Highlands again and that the fund was very low, 'so it will be kind if you will either replenish it, or tell us that it is not to be replenished'. By 5th August he was able to thank Bute for his 'very generous reinforcement of the Second Sight Fund'. On 17th December of the same year Myers was thanking Bute again for being willing to meet the cost of the proposed Ballechin House enquiry.

Myers was enthusiastic and persuasive in his letters to Bute on the subject of Miss Freer,[2] which Dr Campbell has quoted in *Strange Things*. She would prosecute the Second Sight Enquiry, said Myers, in exactly the right spirit, 'a spirit at once scientific and sympathetic'. She had certainly, wrote Myers on 16th August 1894, 'thrown herself heart and soul into the task. I think that sooner or later we shall get a conspectus of the Hebridean mind such as we have never had before.' On 8th October of the same year Myers wrote that he was sure that Bute had 'the right woman and in the right place'. Her experience in the haunted house at Clandon was *capital*, wrote Myers with emphatic underlining, and he was sure that Bute himself must be pleased with Miss Freer's vision of the apparition. He assured Bute that he and Miss Freer would do their

---

[1] The Countess of Caithness was Janet, widow of the sixteenth Earl, whom she had married in 1855. The Duc de Pomar was her second husband, and considerably younger than herself. Both appear in the list of S.P.R. members for the first time in August 1894. The point of Myers' remark seems to be that any money the Countess might bequeath to the S.P.R. was subject to some kind of interest on the part of the Duc de Pomar, who might well survive her and marry again.

[2] This praise of Miss Freer by Myers, of which there was a good deal, did not continue after the quarrel in the Spring of 1897 between Myers and Miss Freer over Miss Chaston, the medium who was with Myers at Ballechin, the few later references to Miss Freer in the correspondence being in very different terms. In his belief (which was entirely erroneous) that his old critic Sir James Crichton-Browne had written the famous unsigned letter to *The Times* in June 1897 that sparked off the Ballechin controversy, Myers wrote to Bute, for example, that Miss Freer had virtually betrayed the S.P.R. to Sir James 'so far as in her lay', just as in May he had intimated to Bute that Miss Chaston was very indignant over Miss Freer's attempt to eject her from Ballechin. These strictures and this change of front were not favourably received by Bute.

'very best' with this important case, of which the reader will hear more.

Miss Freer and Lord Bute first met on 30th May 1894 at her suggestion. Myers had recommended her to Bute as the ideal person to undertake the S.P.R. second sight investigation, and Bute had already agreed. Miss Freer evidently decided, however, that it would be in her interests to make the personal acquaintance of Lord Bute, no doubt confident that he would be quickly charmed by her captivating personality. She accordingly wrote to Lord Bute at his London home on 28th May, using Myers' name as a means of introduction, asking for an interview. The two met, and there is no doubt that Bute was greatly impressed. On 4th June, a few days later, the Rev. Peter Dewar wrote in a letter to Lord Bute:

I am very pleased that your Lordship has had an interview with Miss Goodrich-Freer on the subject of her projected tour of the Western Isles, and that you have formed a high opinion of her gifts and graces. I feel considerably relieved to hear that her association with Borderland *does not imply that she is an adherent of Steadism.*

There is no doubt that Miss Freer very soon exerted very considerable influence over Lord Bute. Their large correspondence, her part of which has been fortunately preserved, shows that she was able quickly to arouse his keen interest in *outré* subjects such as astrological horoscopes, crystal-gazing, clairvoyance (including its alleged value in archaeological research, in which Bute was much involved), and in hypnotism. I have been unable to trace any mention in the literature of Miss Freer's possessing hypnotic skill, although an ability in this direction would undoubtedly help to explain her considerable power to influence others virtually at first meeting. Be that as it may, she wrote to Bute on 6th September 1894:

Last week, however, I visited a haunted house where my human sympathies were evoked to the exclusion of the ghostly—and I hypnotized three of the sufferers, whose lives were literally getting blighted by the terror in which they lived—and suggested that they should be deaf and blind to their visitant. Their instant relief was pathetic to witness!

In earlier pages a number of examples have been given of the extraordinary stories about herself with which Miss Freer regaled Lord Bute, with which the correspondence abounds. She wrote on 19th November 1895 to say that Lord Bute's apparition had appeared to her at Holy Trinity Vicarage, Paddington, the home of her friend Constance Moore, where Miss Freer had become a permanent guest. According to a letter from Lord Bute's daughter, the late Lady Margaret MacRae, Miss Freer told Bute that her phantasm would appear to him in the library at Falkland Palace in Fife at 11 a.m. on a specified day. As Lady Margaret put it, however, 'it never came off'. Miss Freer had a paranormal vision of the original Priory in St Andrews,[1] she told Bute in her letter of 9th October 1895, and was able to hear sounds of worship that 'had no objective origin'. On the evening of the same day, in the same location near the ruined Cathedral in St Andrews, she heard voices and the closing of two invisible doors. She added:

Then came the sound of many feet, and a procession passed me walking in single file; I counted 27 tonsured and robed figures. The doors seemed to remain open for them to pass out at the west end of the crypt—then, I think, across a wide passage beyond, and by another door into a lighted building. I could not see in, and I dared not leave my place, lest all should vanish.

This letter of Miss Freer's is of great interest because of the amusing account given by Lady Margaret MacRae to Dr Campbell of the incident. Lord Bute invited Miss Freer to describe in more detail the habit of the monks of pre-Reformation St Andrews. Her answer was incorrect, but she quickly excused her mistake by asserting that the monks seen by her must have been visitors from another community.

In this connexion it is fair to point out that Lady Margaret and the rest of the family, always excepting Lord Bute himself, were somewhat critical of Miss Freer and her claims. In her letters to her mother and brother Lady Margaret usually referred to Miss Freer with amusement as 'dear Ada' or simply 'the Freer'. Writing to Lady Bute on 26th July 1896, after Miss Freer had been entertained on Lord Bute's yacht R.Y.S. *Kittiwake*, she said:

How did dear Ada enjoy her yachting and the Scilly Isles? I hope she won't send her something or other consciousness, or soul, or whatever she sends about, to see us anywhere![2]

It is clear from the correspondence between Lady Margaret and her brother Lord Colum Crichton-Stuart that they found difficulty in

[1] Miss Freer much enjoyed her visits to St Andrews. Like Andrew Lang, I share her affection for the little grey capital of the ancient kingdom of Fife, which has had associations for me over a long number of years. She wrote to Bute, 'What an interesting place this is! The sky and the sea seem to be among the finest of its many fine shows. I never saw a more magnificent sunset, nor a finer sweep of angry surf.'

[2] Three days later, from Tresco in the Scilly Isles, Lady Margaret wrote, 'I have asked here if Miss Freer came some time ago, and they didn't seem to know about her; perhaps she only sent her ghost or soul or whatever it is!'

believing that Miss Freer had any paranormal powers at all. In a letter passed to Dr Campbell and myself for quotation, a letter which throws light on more than one of Miss Freer's activities and upon Lord Bute's financial support for them, Lady Margaret wrote:

I should think the Freer used Father Allan and got to know him deliberately for that purpose. I am afraid I did not like her and should believe the worst. I don't think she had any second sight or vision herself. I do not know about Swanley. I do not remember when she went to Jerusalem, but saw her there well settled in the early 1900s. Of course, as my Father died in 1900 his help would have ceased by then.

There were other opinions. The Hon. Mrs Stirling of Keir, who was a friend of Lord Bute's daughter, wrote to Dr Campbell to describe her visits to Mount Stuart, the seat of the Bute family. While qualifying her recollections as memories sixty years old, she said that although Lord Bute 'was wax in Miss Freer's hands',[1] and had a touching belief in the findings of the S.P.R.,[2] the rest of the family looked upon Miss Freer as a charlatan. Miss Freer, said Mrs

---

[1] Despite her influence over Lord Bute, Miss Freer was evidently unable to destroy his interest in the medium Florence Cook, whose materialization 'Katie King' was endorsed as genuine by the chemist and physicist William Crookes in circumstances which most sensible persons, both then and now, consider were dictated by Miss Cook's physical attractions and not as a result of scientific enquiry. Miss Freer wrote to Bute on this subject on 10th December 1894, 'I have asked Florence Cook's sister-in-law (comparatively quite a decent person) to tell me about Katie King's end, but have not heard yet. I think it is as well that Mr Crookes's interest in her *has* ceased. I don't think that his evidence is of great value in that connection. I think Mr Myers still clings to Mrs Mellon! [Mrs J. B. Mellon, formerly Miss A. Fairlamb, had been exposed by Mr Thomas Shekleton Henry while wearing a mask and muslin drapery, impersonating her materialization 'Cissie' two months previously.] It is all so hideously material. Fancy the prospect of returning from "the Rest that remaineth" to have to upset tables and wind up musical boxes in a milieu which we poor mortals wouldn't condescend to enter. Living or dead, fancy voluntarily associating with Mrs Williams or Florence Cook!' Despite these strictures, the correspondence between Mr James Coates and Lord Bute shows that as late as 1899, before the first of his seizures, Bute was interested in Florence Cook (by then Mrs Corner) coming to Scotland for private sittings. The story of Florence Cook and William Crookes is told in my *The Spiritualists*, London, 1962, and Dr E. J. Dingwall's *The Critics' Dilemma*, Crowhurst, 1966. Lady Williams-Ellis included an excellent short account in her *Darwin's Moon. A Biography of Alfred Russel Wallace*, London, 1966, as does Mr Simeon Edmunds in *Spiritualism: A Critical Survey*, London, 1966.

[2] This was only true of the period to 1897, the year of the Ballechin upheaval, the mysterious affair of Miss Chaston, and the quarrel between Miss Freer and F. W. H. Myers. Bute's opinion of the behaviour of the S.P.R., and of Myers in particular, was made very plain in his letter to Myers of 4th April 1899.

Stirling, 'was regarded as a joke, and not a very good one'. Sir William Huggins, F.R.S., the astronomer, writing to Lord Bute on 9th September 1894, referred sarcastically to a hair which had been sent to Miss Freer in order to test her clairvoyant powers. The test was a failure. Huggins said, 'I am sorry the hair did not act as a more potent charm. I hope the golden colour of the hair will not suggest to Miss Freer to ask for a further loan, but rather to pay up the Falkland one.'[1]

The two principal cases in which Miss Freer and the S.P.R. became embroiled to the extent of attracting fierce criticism were those concerning the supposed haunting of Clandon Park, near Guildford, in Surrey, and Ballechin House, near Dunkeld, in Perthshire, in both of which Bute became involved as Miss Freer's patron. The incidents and the controversies which resulted were of the same sort: the investigation by the S.P.R. of allegedly haunted houses by subterfuge contrary to the wishes or consent of the owners. It is not surprising that the owners of Clandon and Ballechin bitterly resented both the deceit practised upon them and the resultant publicity, which they regarded as highly detrimental to the future value of their property. In the case of Ballechin in particular, the owners intensely and understandably disliked any exposure of family scandals, which the ghost-hunters suggested might be the cause of the hauntings.

It is hardly to be wondered at that such methods earned for the S.P.R., Miss Freer, and Lord Bute a growing unpopularity, which ultimately exploded as a violent public controversy in the columns of *The Times* in June 1897. The printed criticisms were so formidable and unrestrained, as will be seen, that the S.P.R. leaders asserted that the Society had no official connexion with these unfortunate and embarrassing affairs. They were not successful, which is not surprising in view of the evidence which demonstrates that the Society had been deeply involved in both cases from the beginning.

Clandon Park was the property of Lord Onslow.[2] Rumours of its haunting had appeared in the spiritualist magazine *Light* in 1895,[3]

---

[1] Lord Bute was the owner and hereditary keeper of Falkland Palace in Fife. Miss Freer visited Falkland at the end of her Highland tour in 1894 at Lord Bute's invitation, and wrote him a long account of the visions she said she had seen there.

[2] William Hillier Onslow (1853–1911) was the fourth Earl of Onslow, G.C.M.G., P.C., etc. Formerly Under-Secretary of State for the Colonies (1887), Parliamentary Secretary to the Board of Trade (1888), and Governor of New Zealand (1889–92), he was at the time of the Clandon affair Under-Secretary of State for India.

[3] 'Lord Onslow's Haunted House', *Light*, 1895, p. 565.

and in January 1896 Miss Freer wrote an article in *Borderland* about it.[1] The house was let by Lord Onslow at the time, and gossip had been reported from the domestic staff of the tenants, Captain and Mrs Blaine, of the appearance of a female phantom clad in cream-coloured satin. Miss Freer wrote, 'The present writer has had the advantage of being allowed to make some inquiries on the spot on behalf of the Society for Psychical Research, but the amount of evidence so far obtained has not yet justified a formal report to the Society.'[2]

Miss Freer's enquiry was limited to a single visit to Clandon, the unpublished correspondence shows, on 11th December 1895, when she was entertained by Captain and Mrs Blaine overnight. She was accompanied by Mr G. P. Bidder of the S.P.R.[3] In her paper read to the S.P.R. in January 1897 she said, rather typically it may be thought, that her task had been made easier for her by the fact that she had 'been staying in some country houses in the neighbourhood of Clandon, and Mr Bidder was a resident in the same county'. She told Lord Bute in her private correspondence with him that she had obtained an invitation from Mrs Blaine, although in her paper to the S.P.R. she stated that the tenants had not been very ready to give assistance or information in the matter of the haunting, an observation rather contradicted by her letter to Bute of 15th December 1895. She said in this communication that the Blaines had been very kind in giving her every facility for quiet enquiry, adding, however, that 'Mr Bidder's collecting three housemaids to stand in a row and "give evidence" alarmed them back into their shells, and I had to outstay him to restore the balance'.

Miss Freer said that she and the Blaines 'had a bond of sympathy in the stables, and we make ghosts a parenthesis in our talk of horses'. In a later letter in the same month she added that Captain Blaine 'was the best of the lot,—had seen the world and was a gentleman and consequently easier to deal with. One knew his language.' It is of interest to record that Miss Freer told Lord Bute

---

[1] 'The "Ghosts" at Clandon Park', *Borderland*, January 1896, vol. III, pp. 76–7.

[2] *Ibid.*, pp. 76–7. It is interesting that in this early report, published shortly after her first and only visit in December 1895, Miss Freer put 'Ghosts' in sceptical quotation marks, in the same way as she was later to refer to Myers' friend Iris Jessica Chaston as a 'medium'. Its title can usefully be compared with that of her dramatic account published a year later, 'The Spectre at Clandon House [*sic*] as Seen by Miss X', *Borderland*, 1897, vol. IV, pp. 167–9.

[3] Clandon must have been one of the last cases with which Mr Bidder was concerned. He died on 1st February 1896 as a result of an accident in Manchester on 9th January, when he was run over by a horse and van.

that the main evidence came from the servants, with the exception of her own claim to have seen the apparition herself during this single visit, which she said was corroborative of the servants' stories, and could not have been due to expectation.

Miss Freer never visited Clandon again. In her letter to Bute of 19th February 1896 she said that she had ventured to remind Mrs Blaine of her promise of a second invitation, which had not been forthcoming, and that it would be a pity if the enquiry could not be resumed. On 4th March 1896 in a letter to Lady Bute, written during Lord Bute's illness, Miss Freer said that the Blaines had now left Clandon (Lord and Lady Onslow were taking up residence in the house themselves), but that it was still hoped that Myers might be able to obtain further information from them. Miss Freer was not able to make her way into Clandon a second time because of Lord Onslow's firm dislike of this kind of investigation, as will be seen. It may be thought, therefore, that Miss Freer made a good deal more of the case in her later writings and lectures in 1897 than was justified by the opinion expressed in her first account published in *Borderland* in 1896, when she said that the evidence did not justify a report to the S.P.R. at all.

The same *Borderland* article said that Miss Freer's visit to Clandon had been made on behalf of the S.P.R., while in the later accounts after trouble had developed with Lord Onslow, and notably in the S.P.R. *Journal* of February 1897,[1] it was stated that the investigation had been made at the suggestion of Lord Bute. The matter is confused and it is probably not now possible to ascertain the exact truth. It is not in dispute that Miss Freer was mentioning Clandon in her letters to Lord Bute in December 1895, but as their correspondence was regular and considerable, it would have been most unusual if this had not been the case. On the other hand, it seems that Miss Freer did prepare a report of some sort which she sent to F. W. H. Myers during the same month of December 1895, which demonstrates beyond doubt that the S.P.R. was involved in the matter from the beginning. Myers wrote to Bute on New Year's Day 1896:

Miss X's Clandon experience which she has sent to me is capital!— and the whole thing is quite in your *line—the best, it seems, of the large*

---

[1] *Journal*, S.P.R., February 1897, pp. 21–5. This was a report of the 84th General Meeting of the Society at the Westminster Town Hall on Friday, 29th January, with the President, W. Crookes, in the chair. Miss Freer read her paper on Clandon, 'A Passing Note on a Haunted House', to an appreciative audience.

haunted houses with 'fine confused feeling' in the way of possible iniquities of bygone members of historical families. May the 'pretty lady' live long and prosper!

It is reasonable to ask why, if the enquiry was initiated by Bute, as was later suggested after trouble had developed with the formidable Lord Onslow, Miss Freer sent her report to Myers, who did not think it necessary to tell Bute about it for a period of some weeks. This unpublished letter of Myers' also throws some light on the criticisms made over Ballechin that the S.P.R. was not averse from publicizing family scandals in connexion with alleged hauntings, whether feelings were hurt or not. After this first letter to Bute on the subject of Clandon, Myers continued to send him items of news about the case. On 4th March 1896 he emphasized again the importance of Clandon and Miss Freer's vision of the apparition, and on 21st April 1896, in connexion with the attempt to obtain further information from the Blaines, Myers informed Bute that 'meantime the Blaines draw in their horns for fear of the Earl! We must wait awhile and see what happens. I will write if there is any new development.' These letters suggest that it was Myers who was conducting the affair.

After Lord and Lady Onslow had taken up residence at Clandon early in 1896, an unsuccessful attempt was made to obtain permission for Miss Freer to visit the house again. Enclosed with Myers' letter to Bute of 9th April 1896 was a letter dated 7th April to 'My dear Mr Myers' and signed 'Winifred Burghclere'. In this letter Lady Burghclere stated that she could be of no use in regard to the Clandon ghost. It was, she said, 'a sorry subject' with the Onslows, who firmly believed that the ghost was invented during the tenancy of the Blaines. Rather oddly, Myers asked Bute to destroy this letter, but Bute did not do so and it has now been discovered among his papers.

This letter from Lady Burghclere to Myers is perplexing, for it seems to contradict an account by Miss Freer in both the S.P.R. *Journal* of February 1897 and in her second paper on the subject in *Borderland* in April of the same year, in which she said that the approach to Lord Onslow through Lady Burghclere was made by Lord Bute. In support of this statement Miss Freer published a letter from Lord Bute to herself, explaining what had happened, dated 9th August 1896. In this letter Lord Bute said that what he had done was upon the advice of F. W. H. Myers. What had been wanted, he wrote, was the permission of Lord Onslow for Miss Freer, a sensitive, as Lord Bute called her, to visit Clandon and for the S.P.R. to publish a report on the case. Bute said that he wrote to Lady Burghclere, with whom he was acquainted and whose husband was Lord Onslow's brother-in-law, asking if she would approach Lord Onslow on behalf of the S.P.R., to ask if these two requests could be granted. Lord Bute said that he did not keep a copy of his letter to Lady Burghclere. Lord Onslow's answer had been 'disappointing and surprising'. He refused both requests, saying that he had no belief in the haunting, and was anxious to avoid publicity becoming attached to his property. It seems rather odd that Lady Burghclere, having already written on behalf of Myers with complete lack of success, should nevertheless apparently have agreed to make a later approach at the suggestion of Lord Bute.

Lord Onslow's refusal to allow Miss Freer to visit Clandon a second time did not prevent her publishing reports on the case both in *Borderland* and in the S.P.R. *Journal* in 1897. She said that she had visited Clandon during the occupation by the Blaines, who had entertained her without the knowledge of Lord Onslow. She had tea with her hosts in the dusk of an autumn day.[1] When, later, she went upstairs to dress for dinner, Miss Freer claimed to have seen the apparition of a female figure, cloaked and hooded, with a dress showing as gleaming yellowish white satin where the cloak parted. The figure, said Miss Freer, corresponded with the descriptions of other unnamed percipients.[2] The phantom vanished as she approached it. Miss Freer's story attracted much publicity.

There is some evidence to suggest that this story of Miss Freer's was a fabrication. Her single visit to Clandon, as we have seen, had been made on 11th December 1895 in company with Mr G. P. Bidder. There was, however, another guest who is mentioned nowhere in Miss Freer's colourful published accounts. This was the Duke of Richmond and Lennox,[3] who was just the kind of distinguished person with whose name, the reader may think, Miss Freer would have made great play in her story if there had not been some compelling reason for her not to do so.

---

[1] The date of her only visit was 11th December 1895 as has been stated.

[2] The private correspondence discloses that in April 1896 Myers had received a letter from Lord Onslow's secretary to say that Lord Onslow was 'credibly informed that the ghost was due to the maids frightening a footman' during the Blaines' tenancy. This was not revealed in the S.P.R. or *Borderland* reports. In his letter to Bute containing a casual reference to this, Myers said that the story of the footman and the maids did not account for Miss Freer's vision, a suggestion with which the reader may agree.

[3] Sir Charles Henry Gordon-Lennox, K.G., P.C., D.C.L., LL.D. Sixth Duke of Richmond, Duke of Lennox, Earl of March, and Baron Settrington.

The Duke of Richmond wrote to Lord Bute from his house at Guildford on 12th December 1895:

What a pleasant clever woman Miss Freer is! The Blaines asked her to dine and sleep at Clandon last night, and they asked me to come over to dinner to meet her. I found Bidder was staying there too, who is a County Council friend of mine. Owing to Lord Onslow's dislike to a ghost being supposed to appear at his house, the Blaines are very careful to avoid talking about it in public, and they did not wish the fact of Miss Freer's visit being known. So whilst I was there not a word was said about it, and after Miss Freer had sat in the dark in the state bedroom for some time and came back to the drawing room, one tried to glean from her appearance, if she had had any luck.

This morning she has driven over here, and told us that at present she has seen nothing, and that what to her mind is the unsatisfactory thing about it is that no one but servants *has seen the appearance. She is meanwhile making investigation and enquiries amongst the servants who have left, but who were the first people to report what they saw eighteen months ago. She intends to return here next month and stay longer, as she has to go back to town unfortunately this afternoon. She begs me to say that she will write to you tomorrow.*

The Duke of Richmond wrote to Lord Bute again on 26th December 1895:

I have read Miss K's papers which arrived this morning with the greatest interest. Thank you so much for sending them; I am now forwarding them to Miss Freer as requested by you. I do hope she will have an opportunity of going there again before the Blaines give up the house on February 1, when Onslow returns, who said the other day, the first thing he should do, would be to 'clear the ghost out of the house'.

These letters make it plain that on the morning after the only evening she spent at Clandon Miss Freer told the Duke of Richmond that she had seen nothing, which confirms her first published account in *Borderland* in January 1896, when, as we have seen, she initially said that the evidence did not justify a report. The letters of the Duke of Richmond do not confirm at all, it may be thought, Miss Freer's subsequent story about seeing the apparition herself during her single visit to Clandon. They suggest that this alleged experience may have been worked into her later letters to Bute and Myers and into the subsequent reports published both in *Borderland* and in the S.P.R. *Journal* in 1897, to give some support to a case of alleged haunting that would otherwise have depended on mere gossip from the servants' hall.

The publication of the reports in the S.P.R. *Journal* and *Border-land* in February and April 1897 must have justifiably infuriated Lord Onslow. In *Borderland* Miss Freer had been sufficiently impertinent to suggest that he was an obscurantist, obstructing the progress of science.

There is a tide in the affairs of houses and of men, which neglected at the time leads on to the rocks. Lord Onslow lost an opportunity of which he would have done well to avail himself . . . As things stand, the chatter-boxes (and the commercial value of a good many things is in the hands of the chatterbox)—the people who have time to go out to lunch—will soon allow the statement to pass into history, that 'Clandon has been investigated by the S.P.R., but Lord Onslow was afraid to publish the result'.[1]

Lord Onslow took the opportunity two months later to tell his own side of the story. Miss Freer's subsequent enquiry into the alleged haunting of Ballechin House, in which Lord Bute was again in-volved, had caused a considerable controversy in the correspondence columns of *The Times* in the early summer of 1897, of which the reader will hear more. Mrs Caroline Steuart, the wife of the owner of Ballechin House, had written a letter which *The Times* published on 18th June 1897. Mrs Steuart complained that she 'had not the remotest idea that our home was let to other than ordinary tenants', and that it was not within her knowledge that Colonel Taylor and Miss Freer of the S.P.R. had taken Ballechin House for the purpose of ghost-hunting and the publication of a report. Mrs Steuart added:

In my intercourse with them I spoke as one lady to another, never imagining that my private conversations were going to be used for pur-poses carefully concealed from me—a deceit I resent deeply.

Lord Onslow at once wrote in support of Mrs Steuart, his letter being published in *The Times* of 19th June, the following day. He said that he did not wonder that Mrs Steuart was resentful over the deceit practised upon her. He wrote that in the case of Clandon Park he had let his house to tenants who were persuaded by the S.P.R. to allow similar 'researches to be conducted by certain highly impressionable ladies'. Lord Onslow added:

Their hallucinations were published far and wide in the local, London and foreign newspapers, but were fortunately so ludicrous as to excite nothing but ridicule; yet, did I ever again desire to let the place, many an intending tenant might decline to take a house with such a reputation.

[1] *Borderland,* 1897, vol. IV, p. 167.

*I need hardly add that no other person ever heard, saw or dreamt of a
ghost at Clandon. I wish there were some means of making this society
responsible in hard cash for the effects of the light-headed nonsense by
which they depreciate other people's property.*

F. W. H. Myers' letter in reply to Lord Onslow, published in *The
Times* on 22nd June 1897, claimed that the S.P.R. had 'abstained
from publishing the evidence collected on the subject by two of its
members', and that in consequence Lord Onslow's letter seemed
'scarcely fair'. This was feebly evasive, and was not likely to arouse
confidence in the writer's *bona fides*, for Myers refrained from
mentioning that Miss Freer had addressed the 84th General Meeting
of the Society at Westminster Town Hall on 29th January 1897, five
months previously, on her experiences at Clandon, and that her
paper had been printed in the *Journal* of February 1897.

6

MISS FREER AND THE
BALLECHIN INVESTIGATION

NO NOTE upon Ada Goodrich Freer and her activities in psychical research would be complete without some account of the S.P.R. investigation of Ballechin House, 'the most haunted house in Scotland',[1] during which Fr Allan McDonald himself was one of the visitors. This notorious case was the subject of a substantial book by Miss Freer, with the nominal co-authorship of Lord Bute.[2] It has twice been discussed with approval by the late Harry Price,[3] and once with brevity and some scepticism by Dr E. J. Dingwall and myself.[4] A good deal of further information of the greatest interest has since been discovered, however, from two principal sources. First, the previously unpublished letters to Lord Bute from Miss Freer, F. W. H. Myers, Sir James Crichton-Browne, Sir William Huggins, John Milne, Sir John Ritchie Findlay,[5] and some others on the subject of Ballechin have been made available to Dr Campbell and the present writer. Secondly, two copies of Miss Freer's book, extensively annotated by her, have been located and examined.

On 31st January 1931 Miss Freer (then Mrs H. H. Spoer) wrote to Mr John Lewis, the Editor of the *International Psychic Gazette* in London, from St Lukes Hospital, New York, where she had lain ill since Christmas, and where she was to die less than a month later on

---

[1] This phrase was quoted, with some irony, by Mr J. Callendar Ross in *The Times* of 8th June 1897. There can be no doubt that the late Harry Price used Ballechin as a blueprint for his highly successful book, *The Most Haunted House in England*. Following the procedure adopted at Ballechin, he took a tenancy of Borley Rectory and invited observers to stay there to watch and listen for the alleged phenomena, with printed suggestions as to what they might see and hear. The result was that Borley's previous purely local reputation was enlarged until it became 'the most haunted house in England'.

[2] A. Goodrich Freer and John, Marquess of Bute, *The Alleged Haunting of B—— House*, London, 1899. A second, revised edition was published in 1900.

[3] *Poltergeist over England*, London, 1945, pp. 220-8, and *The End of Borley Rectory*, London, 1946, pp. 294-302.

[4] *Four Modern Ghosts*, London, 1958, pp. 15-20.

[5] The son and heir of the owner of *The Scotsman* newspaper. He succeeded his father in 1898, and received a baronetcy in 1925.

24th February 1931. The letter said that she wished to give her personal copy of *The Alleged Haunting of B—— House* to a library that was on a permanent basis, for she regarded it as a valuable document. It was the second edition of 1900, and had been presented by Miss Freer to her prospective husband, Dr H. H. Spoer, on 6th January 1905, the year of their marriage. Miss Freer's letter to Mr Lewis is pasted on to the half-title of the book, with a note by W. A. Marsden of the British Museum that in accordance with her wishes it was deposited in the Department of Printed Books by Mr John Lewis on 24th December 1931.

At the end of the book a cutting is pasted in from the *International Psychic Gazette* of January 1932. The article is headed 'The Haunting of a Highland House. Psychical Researchers on the Trail of a Ghost', and was by the Editor, John Lewis. In it he described how the book came into his hands. Miss Freer had originally concealed under initials the names of most of the persons involved in the Ballechin drama. In this annotated copy, however, as Mr Lewis put it, she had unveiled for the first time many secrets closely guarded for thirty years, by inserting the names of all the actors, and photographs of most of the scenes.

In the National Library of Scotland is a copy of the first edition of *The Alleged Haunting of B—— House,* also annotated by Miss Freer. It came from the library of Lord Rosebery, to whom it had been presented by Lord Bute. Bute had evidently asked Miss Freer to add to the text the names of the persons concerned with Ballechin for the information of Lord Rosebery, for Bute wrote to him on 12th July 1899 to say that he had invited Miss Freer to prepare the book in this way and send it. The photographs of Ballechin House and its grounds, and of some of the investigators, which Miss Freer inserted into the second edition now in the British Museum, are not present in the Rosebery copy, which, however, gains slightly by having been annotated when the events were more freshly in mind.

In the present work I shall give an account of the Ballechin case for the benefit of those who are not familiar with its previous literature, and at the same time record the identities of the persons whose testimony is to be discussed against the background of the new information which is now available. The unpublished correspondence will, I hope, enable me to throw a good deal of new light upon the whole affair and the bitter controversy that the case aroused, and on the personal quarrel between F. W. H. Myers and Miss Freer at this time.

Ballechin House, situated on the River Tay not far from Dunkeld in Perthshire, was the property of an old Highland family named

Steuart. Like many houses of its kind (and especially Borley Rectory) it enjoyed a slight and merely local reputation of being haunted until scandal-mongers and psychical researchers began to interest themselves in it. Although, according to the biographer of Fr R. H. J. Steuart, S.J., a distinguished member of the family, the ghosts of Ballechin were variously described as those of a big black dog, an old white-haired priest, and a woman in white, the later story of the 'wicked major' with which Miss Freer regaled the investigators was more detailed and exciting.

Major Robert Steuart (1806–76) retired from the service of the East India Company in 1850, sixteen years after he had inherited Ballechin House on the death of his father. He never married. He was regarded as an eccentric because of his excessive fondness for dogs, of which he kept a large number at Ballechin, and his belief in spirit return. It was said that he frequently declared that he would haunt Ballechin after his death, probably in the form of a black spaniel of which he was particularly fond. It was alleged that this was the reason why all fourteen dogs belonging to Major Steuart were killed after his death. Scandal linked Major Steuart's name with that of his young housekeeper, Miss Sarah Nicholson, who died at Ballechin on 14th July 1873 at the age of twenty-seven. According to Miss Freer, Major Steuart, on his death three years later, was buried beside Miss Nicholson.[1] On the other hand, when this story received some publicity, Dr J. A. Menzies, who referred to Major Steuart as 'an old and dear friend', wrote to *The Times* to say that there was not the slightest foundation for the story of the affair with the young housekeeper.[2] 'I can readily believe,' wrote Dr Menzies, 'that people who found his straightforward and uncompromising attitude in public affairs disagreeable should dislike him. Eccentric to some extent he was, but it is a calumny to talk of him as the "wicked major".'

Mr J. Callendar Ross, one of the visitors to Ballechin during the S.P.R. investigation and a leader-writer of *The Times*, wrote in the issue of that newspaper of 8th June 1897:

No haunted house is complete without a legend of a crime, or a tragedy, or a badly-spent life, to explain why the ghost walks. In the drawing-room after dinner we listened to our hostess, who is an excellent narrator, expounding the story of the wicked major. It seems that a former proprietor, who died some twenty years ago, had a standing quarrel with

---

[1] *The Alleged Haunting of B—— House*, second edition, 1900, pp. 21–8. Unless otherwise stated, all references will be to this later enlarged edition.
[2] *The Times*, 21st June 1897.

Mrs Grundy. He kept his house full of dogs; he did not care for the society of his neighbours; he was rather feared than loved; and local gossip, with reason or without, charged him with unnecessary familiarity with his housekeeper.

Sir James Crichton-Browne, F.R.S., who went to Ballechin with Mr Callendar Ross, wrote:

The legend as to the origin of the haunting of B. was told to us by Miss Freer. It appeared that some twenty years ago the proprietor of B. was a retired major of eccentric habits, who kept the house full of dogs, would have nothing to do with his neighbours, was accused of wicked conduct, and was generally feared.[1]

Miss Freer said on p. 31 of her book that 'there seems to have been no idea of the place being haunted before the deaths of Sarah N—— and of Major S——, whereas since that time the peculiar phenomena have been constantly attested'.

According to Miss Freer, Lord Bute first heard about Ballechin and its ghosts in August 1892, when a priest, Fr Patrick Hayden, S.J., visited Falkland Palace in Fife, of which Bute was the owner and hereditary keeper. Fr Hayden had been staying at Ballechin during the previous month of July, and had heard strange noises and had seen, between waking and sleeping, a momentary vision of a brown crucifix.[2] A year later, in August 1893, Fr Hayden met a Miss Yates, who twelve years previously had been a governess at Ballechin and had left because 'so many people complained of queer noises in the house'.[3] Fr Hayden reported this story to Lord Bute.

In 1896 Ballechin House was let for three months to a naturalized Spaniard, Mr Joseph R. Heaven, of Kiftsgate Court, Mickleton, Gloucestershire, and his family.[4] Mr Heaven wrote to *The Times* during the controversy:

When I went to Ballechin at the beginning of August my family had already been there a few days, and at once they told me they had found out the house was supposed to be haunted and that they had heard most unaccountable noises. I had the greatest difficulty to persuade my people to stay in the place, and after all we left Scotland about the end of September—two months earlier than usual. I personally did not

---

[1] *The Doctor's After Thoughts*, London, 1932, p. 177.
[2] *The Alleged Haunting of B—— House*, pp. 1–10. [3] *Ibid.*, pp. 10–12.
[4] In a letter to Lord Bute of 21st July 1899 Miss Freer wrote with Victorian insularity of the Heavens that they were 'pleasant and intelligent, and what in English folk would be "barbarous opulence jewel-thick" is less offensive in foreigners'. Their Spanish name was Cielo.

give any importance to the rumours that Ballechin-house is haunted, and attributed the very remarkable noises heard to the hot-water pipes and the peculiar way in which the house is built. In fact, I have to confess I cannot believe in ghosts, and consequently I did my best to persuade everybody that Ballechin was not haunted, but I am afraid I was not always successful.[1]

Mr Heaven's lack of belief in the ghosts of Ballechin and his opinion that the noises were due to the hot-water pipes and the peculiar construction of the house is hard to reconcile with the story of one of his guests, a Mrs Howard, who published her experiences in a magazine article on 9th October 1896 and whom Miss Freer quoted at length on pp. 58–62 of her book:

The haunted room (for so I may justly call it) was inhabited by two or three persons in succession, who were so alarmed and disturbed by the violent knockings, shrieks, and groans which they heard every night, and which were also heard by many others along the same corridor, that they refused to sleep there after the first few nights . . . Even the dogs cannot be coaxed into this room, and if forced into it, they crouch with marked signs of fear. The disturbances take place between 12 and 4.30, and never at any other time. A young lady, of by no means timid disposition, and possessed of great presence of mind, has often heard the swing-door pushed open and footsteps coming along the corridor, pausing at the door. She has frequently looked out and seen nothing. The footsteps she has also heard in her room, and going round her bed. Many persons have had the same experiences, and many have heard the wild unearthly shriek which has rung through the house in the stillness of the night . . . As I write, at the commencement of October, the house on the lonely hillside is deserted; the tenants have gone southwards; an old caretaker (too deaf to hear the weird sounds which nightly awaken the echoes) is the sole occupant. Even she closes up all before dusk, and retires into her quarters below; though she hears not, her sight is un-impaired, and she perhaps dreads to meet the hunchback figure which is said to glide up the stairs, or the shadowy form of a grey lady who paces with noiseless footfall the lonely corridor, and has been seen to pass through the door of one of the rooms. Within the last two months a man

[1] *The Times*, 14th June 1897. On p. 15 of her book Miss Freer said of the Heaven tenancy that Ballechin, with the shooting, was let 'for a year, to a wealthy family of Spanish origin. Their experience was of such a nature that they abandoned the house at the end of seven weeks, thus forfeiting the greater part of their rent, which had been paid in advance.' This was a gross exaggeration, as will be seen from Mr Heaven's letter, which suggests that he might have stayed for a maximum period of four months in normal circumstances. In the earlier part of his letter he refers to 'my tenancy for three months last year'.

*with bronzed complexion and bent figure has been seen by two gentle-
men, friends of mine. They both describe him as having come through
the door and passed through the room in which they were, about three in
the morning.*

Miss Freer said that Mrs Howard's story was in no sense 'written
up', and that it was in any event entirely corroborated by other
evidence.[1] I have found little confirmation of this. Two of Mrs
Howard's fellow guests at Ballechin were a Colonel Aitchieson and a
Major Berkeley. They are picturesquely referred to in her account
as witnesses, although not by name:

*Those who serve under her Majesty's colours are proverbially brave;
they will gladly die for their country, with sword in hand and face to the
foe.*

Major Berkeley wrote to the Hon. Everard Feilding in January
1897, confirming the fact of the noises at Ballechin, but nothing
else:

*Between two and four in the morning there used to be noises on the door
(of Colonel Aitchieson's room) as if a very strong man were hitting the
panels as hard as ever he could hit, three times in quick succession—a
pause, and then three times again in quick succession, and perhaps
another go. It was so loud that I thought it was on the door of his
dressing-room, but he said he thought it was on his bedroom door. One
theory is, that it was the hot water in the pipes getting cold, which, I
am told, would make a loud throbbing noise. I tripped out pretty quick
the first time I heard it, but could see nothing. Of course it is broad day-
light in Scotland then.*

*The same banging was, I believe, heard on one of the bedroom doors
down the passage, in the wing on the ground floor, and on investigation
I found there were hot-water pipes outside that door as well. There were
yarns innumerable while I was there about shrieks and footsteps heard,
and bedclothes torn off. But I did not experience these.*

Colonel Aitchieson corroborated this account in a letter to Major
Berkeley:

*You write asking me about Ballechin House and its spook. Well, I never
saw anything, and what I heard was what you heard, a terrific banging
at one's bedroom door, generally from about 2 to 3 a.m., about two nights*

---

[1] *The Alleged Haunting of B—— House*, p. 58. She did not reveal that in her
letter to Lord Bute of 15th July 1897 she had said that 'Mrs Howard will not
corroborate her statement to me as to the most interesting of Mr Howard's
experiences'.

out of three. Of course there were other yarns of things heard, etc., but I personally never heard or experienced anything else than this banging at the door, which I could never account for.

These two accounts, read in conjunction with that of Mr Heaven, suggest that both Mrs Howard's story and that told by Mr Harold Sanders in *The Times* of 21st June 1897 of the events at Ballechin in the autumn of 1896 should be accepted with reserve. Sanders, a butler formerly in the employ of Mr Heaven, had been at Ballechin during the family's stay there. He wrote:

One gentleman (a colonel) told me he was awakened on several occasions with the feeling that some one was pulling the bed clothes off him;[1] *sometimes heavy footsteps were heard, at others like the rustling of a lady's dress; and sometimes groans were heard, but nearly always accompanied by heavy knocking . . . I then retired to my bed, but not to sleep, for I had not been in bed three minutes before I experienced the sensation as before, but, instead of being followed by knocking, my bed-clothes were lifted up and let fall again—first at the foot of my bed, but gradually coming towards my head; I held the clothes around my neck with my hands, but they were gently lifted in spite of my efforts to hold them. I then reached around me with my hand, but could feel nothing. This was immediately followed by my being fanned as though some bird was flying around my head, and I could distinctly hear and feel some-thing breathing on me. I then tried to reach some matches that were on a chair by my bedside, but my hand was held back as if by some invisible power. Then the thing seemed to retire to the foot of my bed. Then I suddenly found the foot of my bed lifted up and carried around towards the window for about three or four feet; then replaced to its former position. All this did not take, I should think, more than two or three minutes, although at the time it seemed hours to me. Just then the clock struck four, and, being tired out with my long night's watching, I fell asleep. This, Mr Editor, is some of my experiences while at Ballechin.*[2]

My view is that the evidence of Mr Heaven, Colonel Aitchieson, and Major Berkeley demonstrates that mysterious noises were frequently heard in Ballechin House, but there is no independent support for the accounts by Sanders of the pulling of bedclothes and the holding of his hand 'as if by some invisible power', nor of Mrs

---

[1] Colonel Aitchieson and Major Berkeley were the only military members of Mr Heaven's house party. It will be seen that Colonel Aitchieson's unpublished personal account suggests that this incident was probably invented by Sanders. It is interesting to compare Colonel Aitchieson's story of the banging on the door with Professor Balfour-Browne's recollection of the boot marks, see p. 87.

[2] *The Times*, 21st January 1897.

Howard's stories of the hunchback figure, the grey lady, and the man with the bronzed complexion and bent figure. What caused the noises is a matter of opinion. Dr E. J. Dingwall and I have previously and briefly commented upon them in another place.[1] In this connexion the published view of Professor John Milne, F.R.S.,[2] the distinguished seismologist, is of great interest. In a letter published in *The Times* of 21st June 1897 at the height of the Ballechin House controversy, Milne wrote:

I am more inclined to the view that the Ballechin mysteries are to be explained not so much from the character of the noises which have been heard, but rather from the knowledge we possess relating to the seismicity of the district in which they have been recorded. For years past this part of Perthshire has been well known as the hotbed for British earthquakes. Between 1852 and 1890 no less than 465 shocks have been noted there, out of which number 430 are claimed by Comrie. Many of these have been accompanied by sounds and often, as is common in earthquake countries and as I can testify from considerable personal experience, sounds may be heard and no movement can be either felt or recorded by an ordinary seismograph. As early as 1840 the British Association appointed a committee to investigate the Perthshire earthquakes, and instruments were established in the Parish Church at Comrie. In one of the reports of this committee we find a letter from David Milne to the Rev. Dr. Buckland, in which he relates the experience of Lady Moncrieff, who stated that whilst residing in Comrie-house scarcely a day passed without hearing either the rumbling noise in the earth or the moaning in the air produced by a mysterious agent. Many other quotations might be made to show that in Perthshire seismic sounds have been common,[3] and, because such sounds do not travel far from their origin, they might be heard at an isolated house in the country and nowhere else . . . The Society for Psychical Research when on bogey-hunting expeditions might possibly find that the suggested use of tromometric apparatus might not only lay home-made ghosts but would furnish materials of value to all who are interested in seismic research.

The reader now has before him the story of the alleged haunting of Ballechin House prior to the S.P.R. investigation in 1897. The

---

[1] *Four Modern Ghosts*, pp. 17–19.

[2] In 1897 Milne was Secretary of the Seismological Committee of the British Association, a position he occupied until his death in 1913.

[3] Comrie is about 22 miles from Ballechin. The latter lies in the triangle formed by Pitlochry (3 miles distant), Dunkeld (9 miles distant), and Aberfeldy (6 miles distant), all three of which have an earthquake history. Charles Davison, *A History of British Earthquakes*, Cambridge, 1924, pp. 62 and 159.

first firm intention to conduct an enquiry at this time is mentioned in a letter from Myers to Lord Bute dated 17th December 1896. Myers said that he had 'received the papers re the Perthshire haunted house: and I am doing my best to find someone willing to go there'. It is clear that Bute had expressed a willingness to pay the cost of an S.P.R. investigation, for Myers said that since this was so, he anticipated no difficulty in obtaining volunteers to stay in the house. This optimism was well founded, and on Myers' recommendation Ballechin was occupied by Miss Freer, her friend Miss Constance Moore, and Colonel G. L. le Mesurier Taylor from early February 1897 to the middle of May. Colonel Taylor was a prominent member of both the Society for Psychical Research and the London Spiritualist Alliance. Lord Bute paid all the expenses, and the house was staffed with servants.

The tenancy, which was a furnished one, was negotiated in Colonel Taylor's name by agents who were instructed that the house was required by Colonel Taylor and his family, with 'a little winter shooting and some good spring fishing', as was later revealed during the controversy in a letter printed in *The Times* of 16th June 1897 from Colonel Taylor's own agents, Messrs T. and J. Speedy of Edinburgh. This embarrassed communication was in response to an indignant letter, also printed in *The Times* on the same day,[1] from the agents for the owners, Messrs R. H. Moncrieff and Co. of Edinburgh. In their letter Messrs Moncrieff complained that the offer to rent Ballechin House had been accepted on the understanding that Colonel Taylor required the property for his personal occupation with the rabbit shooting and fishing, neither the S.P.R. nor the real purpose for which Ballechin House was to be used, ghost-hunting, having been so much as hinted at in the negotiations. Messrs Moncrieff indignantly concluded their letter:

The damage and injury done to Captain Steuart in the whole matter will be far-reaching and irreparable, and we have on his behalf to intimate that he will hold all those concerned responsible for the loss and damage he is bound to sustain.[2]

Unless a number of persons were to be disbelieved, it would seem that the negotiations by the S.P.R. representatives for the tenancy of Ballechin House were lacking in frankness. Captain J. M. S. Steuart wrote to *The Times* from Paris on 10th June 1897 and his

[1] Messrs Moncrieff and Co. published the whole of the correspondence relating to the letting of Ballechin House in *The Times* on 16th June 1897 in support of their statement that they had been deceived.

[2] *The Times*, 16th June 1897.

letter was printed on 14th June, two days before his agents published the facts. He wrote:

As owner of Ballechin, I desire to state that I had no idea I was letting Ballechin to Lord Bute and the Psychical Society, and would never have done so had I known. I let Ballechin for three months to a Colonel Taylor, with fishing, etc., and it was only at the end of his tenancy I discovered for what purposes and by whom Ballechin had been really rented.

The letter published in *The Times* of 18th June 1897, in which Mrs Caroline Steuart wrote that she deeply resented the deceit that had been practised upon her, has already been quoted in connexion with the Clandon affair. In regard to the reassuring description of Colonel Taylor as a family man interested in shooting and fishing, which his own agents Messrs T. and J. Speedy said had been represented to them, Miss Freer herself disclosed the truth two years later in her book. In trying to support her unlikely assertion that Messrs Moncrieff, the agents for the Steuart family, should have been aware that Colonel Taylor was 'well known as a Spiritualist in England and America', she incautiously revealed that Colonel Taylor 'neither shoots nor fishes', and that he was a widower without family.[1]

In regard to the general involvement of the S.P.R. in the affair from the beginning, which is made perfectly clear by Myers' correspondence, it is of interest to record that Miss Freer said in her book that if Colonel Taylor had not agreed to have the lease put in his name, then either William Crookes, the President of the S.P.R., or Mr Arthur Smith, the Society's Hon. Treasurer, would have done so.[2] And as for Myers' promotion of the affair and his desire and recommendation that she should go to Ballechin, Miss Freer said that Myers 'wrote urgently to her' saying that if she did not get phenomena at Ballechin probably nobody would.[3]

Miss Freer and her friends doubtless found living at Ballechin, with a staff of servants at their disposal and all expenses paid, pleasant enough. Lord Bute described it as 'a luxurious country house, ample, though not too large, in a beautiful neighbourhood'.[4] Miss Freer herself, in a diary which she kept of her stay in the house, said:

[1] *The Alleged Haunting of B—— House*, pp. 75–6.
[2] *Ibid.*, p. 74.
[3] *Ibid.*, p. 76.
[4] *Ibid.*, p. 81. This part of Perthshire may indeed be considered the best favoured district of the Scottish Highlands.

It is cheerful, sunny, convenient, healthy, and built on a very simple plan, which admits of no dark corners or mysteries of any kind. A pleasanter house to live in I would not desire, but it is constructed for summer rather than for winter use.[1]

During the tenancy a number of persons, between thirty and forty in all, were invited to stay at Ballechin for a few nights at a time to experience the alleged phenomena which, as we have seen, had been variously reported in the past as including strange noises, objective manifestations, such as the lifting of beds and bedclothes, the appearance of several spectres of various kinds, and a vision of a crucifix. The distinguished visitors included Professor Oliver Lodge, Andrew Lang, the Hon. Everard Feilding, Archbishop Angus MacDonald,[2] Sir James Crichton-Browne, Fr Allan McDonald, John Ritchie Findlay, Rev. Charles J. M. Shaw, and F. W. H. Myers, the latter in company with a young woman from London, Miss Jessica Iris Chaston, described scornfully by Miss Freer in her book as 'a "medium"'.[3]

It is of great interest that today, eighty years after the Ballechin controversy, new evidence is available from the unpublished papers of Lord Bute throwing fresh light on the mystery. Two letters, substantial in length and written privately to Lord Bute by men of intelligence and substance who were visitors to the house during the S.P.R. tenancy, have been made available to Dr Campbell and myself. One, Mr H. F. Cadell, W.S., an Edinburgh solicitor who had acted for Colonel Taylor in regard to the formalities of the tenancy, had experiences during his stay. The other, Mr (later Sir) John Ritchie Findlay, the son and heir of the owner of *The Scotsman*, had none, but his letter is of considerable value because it contains his private appraisal to Lord Bute of some of the principal persons involved in the Ballechin investigation carried out by the S.P.R.

Mr Cadell, writing to Lord Bute on 8th March 1897 from 19 Ainslie Place, Edinburgh, said:

I went to Ballechin on Saturday last and Mrs Macphail has suggested that I should write to you about what occurred there, during my stay. It was arranged that I was to sleep in Room No. 2, and Colonel Taylor in No. 3—No. 1 being empty. I went to bed about 12 o'clock. I suddenly awoke with the impression that there was someone in the room. I lay still and tried to realise what was in the room but could not do so. There was

---

[1] *The Alleged Haunting of B—— House*, p. 84.
[2] R.C. Archbishop of St Andrews and Edinburgh, formerly Bishop of Argyll and the Isles.
[3] *Ibid.*, p. 184.

no idea of movement in my mind, but I felt convinced that someone was there. This impression appeared to gradually fade out of my mind after about seven or ten minutes, and I then got up and looked at my watch. The time was 4.40 a.m. I then went back to bed, but did not go to sleep—I heard the clock on the main stairs strike 5.

Shortly after I thought I heard someone moving in No. 1, which I knew to be empty. I listened and I thought someone seemed to be moving round three sides of the room and then coming back again. The movement went on for 3 or 4 minutes and then stopped, but after a pause of some minutes it commenced again. I tried to make out footsteps, and could not do so. The movement was that of a heavy body going round the room, and the floor seemed to shake, as old flooring will when a heavy man walks about. My bed also was shaken. After going on for some time the movement stopped and again after a pause began again. I heard the movements four separate times. The periods for which the movements and the pauses lasted were irregular. After waiting some time and finding that the noises seemed to have stopped altogether, I got up and lit the candle at 5.25 and read for 25 minutes, when I felt sleepy and blew out the candle. I did not however go to sleep, but heard six strike. The day was then dawning. I noticed that the rooks began making a noise about 5.35.

About ten minutes after the clock struck six, I heard a noise like a lightfooted person running down stairs, which seemed to adjoin No. 3, where Colonel Taylor was sleeping, and almost immediately after I heard a loud rapping at the door of No. 1. Then there was a momentary pause, and as I jumped out of bed the rapping occurred again. As I opened the door of my room leading into the passage the rapping occurred again but less loudly. There was no one in the passage, and I went back to bed having shut the door. No sooner had I got into bed than there was a knock at my door, which I thought must be Colonel Taylor coming to speak to me on account of the rapping at No, 1. I therefore called out 'Come in', but there was no answer, and I accordingly went to the door again, only to find no one there.

I heard the servants in the bedrooms above me get up about 6.30, and as 7 struck I heard them moving about the house. Colonel Taylor did not hear anything. There are no stairs coming down to the bedroom storey, where I thought I heard footsteps. The rapping was not in any way an alarming noise. 'Ouija' [1] had informed us that I was not to be disturbed, and I was not therefore 'expecting'. That night it referred to 'the Major' and stated that he formerly occupied Rooms No. 3 & 8. I could not therefore have expected noises in No. 1.

Last night I was not so much disturbed, but I awoke at 3.10 and did

[1] It is reasonable to conclude that Miss Freer was the operator.

not sleep after that. I had the same sensation as on the preceding night that whenever I was going to sleep something woke me. At 5.20 I heard three noises very close together, but they were very distant, and sounded from the direction of No. 8.

Everybody in the house has heard noises with the exception of Colonel Taylor. The Butler was an unbeliever until Saturday night, when he heard something that appears to have convinced him.

I was very much interested in what I heard, and I have to thank your Lordship for the opportunity of going to Ballechin.

P.S. I forgot to mention that I do not believe in the screams, which former tenants assert that they have heard. No one has heard them during this year. I heard the owls last night, and in the night their hoots do not sound unlike screams. I am sure there must be two stories in connection with the place—one which has to do with 'the Major', and the other of older date with all sorts of personages connected with it. I ought also perhaps to mention that after hearing the noises at No. 1, I went down the main stair and came back up the back stair. H.F.C.

Mr Findlay wrote to Lord Bute on 3rd March 1897 from 3 Rothesay Terrace, Edinburgh. In a previous short note he had expressed his appreciation of the hospitality afforded him during his stay. He had deliberately slept in Bedroom No. 3, in which both Fr Hayden and Major Berkeley had heard strange noises, but his own experiences 'were absolutely nil'. He added 'that as all that is worth relating rests almost entirely on the testimony of Miss Freer', he did not feel that anything could usefully be printed in *The Scotsman* for the present. Lord Bute had evidently responded to Mr Findlay's first note by sending some papers dealing with the earlier evidence for the haunting. In reply Mr Findlay wrote:

I am much obliged to you for sending me the documents which I return. Some of them Mr Shaw had already shown me but the most of them are new.

In writing before I refrained from indicating what opinion I had formed of the Ballechin investigations, but your letters encourage me to think that it may be of some interest to you to know how they impressed a critical and somewhat sceptical observer. I may say that my natural instinct would be to find a personal explanation of the various phenomena; and to explain the 'ouija' messages as the result of such sub-consciousness as Binet has investigated. I am neither nervous nor susceptible to impressions. I am prepared to be told that this amounts to a preconception, which invalidates my testimony, but I submit that it is not more illogical than the desire to see and hear which seemed to be common to most at Ballechin. It is perhaps impossible really to approach any subject with an absolutely empty mind.

I may tell you frankly, though in confidence, that there was hardly a person at Ballechin whose testimony I should set much store by in matters of the kind. They could not stand cross-examination, and in the eyes of common men their testimony would be vitiated by predisposition and inclination. Miss Freer you know better than I do. She knows what she is about, but she is an expert in such matters, and her personal tendencies or 'powers' cannot be ignored. Colonel Taylor is a professed spiritualist—a man of sound common sense but little imagination. He has had no 'experiences' but if he should have any, a supernatural explanation would be the first that would suggest itself, and he would accept it with an alacrity that would only amuse most people.

Mr Powles[1] was I think the most nervous man I ever met. He seems to live in a world of influences, which are a perpetual source of annoyance to him. He can tell by instinct whether a room or house is haunted and his instinct is confirmed by his experience. He sees nothing but is prepared by constitution to feel and hear. Mr Shaw the parson,[2] on the other hand, is in the habit of seeing figures outlined in light against a dark background. These he told me he could see at will. He seems to have little critical instinct, and a thorough belief in the supernatural. The first night I was there he went down the avenue in order that he might see the apparition of the nun. He went predisposed to see and he did see what he described as 'something'. The following incident illustrates his attitude of mind. Miss Freer came to meet me in a waggonette. The horse started at the train, and she was thrown out. He saw all that happened, yet he seriously asked her if she thought she had been thrown out by supernatural agencies. These things should be kept in view in dealing with his testimony.

Miss Langton is a young girl, somewhat hysterical, not strong physically, and strangely susceptible to outside influences. Miss Moore on the other hand struck me as being a person of sound common sense, and her evidence I should value beyond that of all the others who are predisposed by temperament to such experiences. Of course it may be said that it is only persons of this sort, who are competent to investigate such matters, but if you adopt this position you must abandon all hope of convincing the majority of mankind, who I am afraid have little sympathy with such an attitude of mind.

With regard to the sounds heard I can offer no explanation. They may be natural sounds formalised and exaggerated by the imagination of those

---

[1] Mr Lewis Charles Powles was an Associate of the S.P.R.
[2] Rev. Charles J. M. Shaw was an Associate of the S.P.R.

who heard them. But in the absence of any personal experience I do not put this forward with any confidence.

With regard to the 'ouija' messages I have less difficulty. From your letter I gather that you are inclined to halt between two opinions, the one that they are subconscious dreams, the other that they are communications from a mischievous and ignorant spirit. What strikes me forcibly about them, is their groping and tentative character. The dates have gradually been brought down to present times. It must too, be borne in mind that on the part of those who have been obtaining them there has been a constant effort to verify them by tradition and documents. Burke's Landed Gentry was constantly referred to. The minds of those engaged were thus fixed upon what is true in them and this would almost certainly lead to the elaboration in a halting fashion of a story which bears a strong resemblance to the truth. Another feature of them is that I can find little or nothing of importance in them, which I did not know to be consciously or unconsciously in the minds of those engaged. The Scottish use of 'West' had been discussed when I was there, yet its use in a subsequent 'ouija' message is considered matter for surprise. Similarly the phrase 'ora pro nobis' was in the mind of Mr Shaw. Another criticism which suggests itself is the manner of indicating time, e.g. 10.53. This is of quite modern origin, and even now is not in use among uneducated persons unless they are railway servants. How does the use of this phrase fit in with the hypothesis of an ignorant spirit? In the messages of earlier date, it is a sort of anachronism of the kind that vitiates a document.

Were those at Ballechin kept in absolute ignorance of all the details of family history I should have more confidence in the 'ouija' messages. The date 1880 puzzles me. I have done nothing, and will do nothing to enlighten them as to the details contained in your letters.

I would not have ventured to criticise so freely a party with whom I spent two very pleasant days unless I had thought it might interest you to learn how these things struck an outsider. This too is my only excuse for troubling you with a letter of such length.

I would like very much to go back if I could manage it.

With many thanks for being allowed to read the documents you sent me.

There is another opinion which is not so valuable as those of Mr Cadell and Mr Findlay, merely because it is a recollection recorded now, after an interval of seventy years. It is, however, of the greatest interest; not only because Professor W. A. F. Balfour-Browne is a distinguished entomologist, trained originally as a barrister, whose remarkable memory is well known among his colleagues, but because he is almost certainly the only surviving person who, as a young man of twenty-three, was a visitor at Ballechin during those far-off days of the S.P.R. investigation.[1] On p. 210 of her book Miss Freer describes how near the end of the tenancy Ballechin was visited by Sir James Crichton-Browne, his nephew and a friend. Sir James's nephew was Mr W. A. F. Balfour-Browne of Magdalen College, Oxford, and his friend was Mr J. Callendar Ross, a leader-writer for *The Times*. Dr Campbell has had the privilege of meeting and corresponding with Professor Balfour-Browne, who wrote to him on 29th September 1966:

I knew nothing about the matter until my uncle asked me to accompany him to Ballechin. I think I had just come down from Oxford.

The haunted house was a large one and we three enquirers were bedded in one end of it in three rooms which connected with one another, I having the middle one. I remember my uncle's activity in moving a large wardrobe which covered the door from his room to mine. For the few nights we were there all was peace but one interesting item occurs to me. We three came down to breakfast one morning and only Miss Freer's companion was down, and in answer to our enquiries, she said that all had been quiet at the end of the house where she and Miss Freer slept. Later Miss Freer told us that the ghost seemed to have moved to her end of the house on the previous night!

We examined the whole house, and except for marks on various doors indicating that someone had hit them with some object, such as boots, there was nothing out of the way except that, all round the top floor rooms there was a passage round the house. I managed to crawl along this passage and again arrive at the small door by which I had got into it. The passage might have enabled someone to play ghosts upon the servants or whoever slept in those top rooms and the boot-marks suggested that there had been some joking. Except for these possibilities, it was suggested that the house lay upon a line which had shown signs of earth movement. I need not tell you the impression that my uncle and Mr Ross got of the matter but I felt that Miss Freer had either been sent there to prove the existence of a ghost or she herself had decided to do so on her own authority.

I know nothing about Ross except that someone told me he was a leader-writer for The Times. *I never heard of any of the other people you mention. If the row about Miss Chaston was a matter of morals it is possible that I was regarded as too young to be told about it!"*

As in the case of the alleged haunting of Clandon, within a short time of her arrival at Ballechin Miss Freer claimed to see an

[1] Professor Balfour-Browne died on 28th September 1967 at the age of 93.

apparition, this time of a nun, in a glen near the house one evening in February. Neither of her companions, the Hon. Everard Feilding and Mr Lane Fox, could see anything, a failure which Miss Freer attributed to their temperamental unsuitability for experiences of this kind.[1] Miss Freer was, as we know, an automatic writer, a class of person in whom the S.P.R. was to become increasingly interested from the turn of the century to the present time. She soon obtained information through her 'ouija board' that the name of the nun was 'Ishbel'. She also heard 'Ishbel' speak and weep, and was able to describe her in some detail in a letter to Lord Bute:

'Ishbel' appears to me to be slight, and of fair height. I am unable, of course, to see the colour of her hair, but I should describe her as dark. There is an intensity in her gaze which is rare in light-coloured eyes. The face, as I see it, is in mental pain, so that it is perhaps hardly fair to say that it seems lacking in that repose and gentleness that one looks for in the religious life. Her dress presents no peculiarities. The habit is black, with the usual white about the face, and I have thought that when walking she showed a lighter under-dress. She speaks upon rather a high note, with a quality of youth in her voice. Her weeping seemed to me passionate and unrestrained.[2]

A few days later Miss Freer began to see another apparition in company with that of 'Ishbel', referred to in her account as 'Marget' and heard the two figures conversing in the glen.[3] On a later occasion in company with Miss Freer, her friend Miss Langton heard the sound of low conversation, and Miss Moore heard 'a murmuring voice'.[4] Another visitor, the Rev. Charles J. M. Shaw, saw the figure in the glen on 19th February, and heard a loud groan and saw a momentary vision of a crucifix on the wall of his bedroom at Ballechin on 24th February.[5] On 26th February Miss Freer saw the apparition of a woman with a 'coarsely handsome' face in the drawing-room.[6]

It has to be remembered that in investigations of this kind in allegedly haunted localities the power of suggestion is exceedingly strong. Colonel Taylor himself observed in a latter to Lord Bute:

The clairvoyant visions of 'Ishbel' in the grounds are not of great evidential value for the scientific world in general, and I think that any amount of 'voices' could be read into the noises of the running stream, near where she is seen, by those who 'wished to hear'.[7]

---

[1] *The Alleged Haunting of B—— House*, p. 92.
[2] *Ibid.*, p. 93.   [3] *Ibid.*, pp. 101–2.   [4] *Ibid.*, p. 108.
[5] *Ibid.*, pp. 112–13 and 121–4.   [6] *Ibid.*, p. 126.   [7] *Ibid.*, p. 145.

The tendency of perfectly honest but impressionable persons, under strong suggestion from a dominating character, towards small hallucinatory experiences is documented in my essay on D. D. Home in my *New Light on Old Ghosts*. I have never doubted Miss Freer's ability to influence those with whom she came in contact. The Rev. C. J. M. Shaw, moreover, was not only an Associate of the S.P.R., but was also a member of one of the spiritualist circles subscribing to the occult magazine she organized and sub-edited.[1]

While all this was going on, Miss Freer's colleague Colonel Taylor unfortunately heard and saw nothing to which he attached any psychical significance, although he repeatedly slept in the most haunted bedroom and paid many visits to the glen hoping to see the phantom nuns. Miss Freer said that this was because 'although a frequent visitor to haunted houses, he has never had any experience'.[2] Colonel Taylor left Ballechin on 16th March, after spending five weeks there 'very pleasantly', as he wrote in his letter to Lord Bute on 19th March 1897. Colonel Taylor went on to say, surprisingly in the circumstances, that he was disappointed in the way in which the 'ghostly influence' at Ballechin had manifested itself during his stay. He thought the vision of the brown crucifix was important, but expressed some scepticism in regard to the whole of the rest of the phenomena. He added:

It is very interesting to note Miss Freer's experiences but in regard to those of others who have something to relate, it is perhaps difficult to determine how much these statements should be discounted for error of observation and self-suggestion. I heard many noises in the night during my stay at B——, but they were of much the same sort I have been accustomed to hear at a similar time in other houses. I think that some of our witnesses may have given them undue prominence, under the influence of their own expectancy.

My discussion of the alleged haunting of Ballechin is intended to be no more than the placing before the reader of some hitherto unpublished information, and to be an introduction to the surprising events that quickly followed the end of the S.P.R. investigation in May 1897. The reader will no doubt have formed a preliminary opinion of the 'phenomena' at Ballechin. In this connexion a comment made by Frank Podmore in his review[3] of the *Alleged Haunting of B—— House* in S.P.R. *Proceedings* is not lacking in interest. It is

---

[1] 'Our Circles and Members', *Borderland*, 1895, vol. II, pp. 88–92. Mr Shaw's name appears on p. 90.
[2] *The Alleged Haunting of B—— House*, p. 140.
[3] *Proceedings*, S.P.R., 1900–1, vol. XV, pp. 98–100.

true that the Society decided to disclaim Ballechin and throw Miss Freer to the wolves when the storm broke in the columns of *The Times* in June 1897, and that an adverse review could therefore be expected. It was, however, valid for Podmore to say, as he did, that it was somewhat significant that during the investigation it was Miss Freer who first heard the noises, who first saw the apparition, and who was most frequently and most conspicuously favoured with 'phenomena'.

7

MISS FREER AND THE
BALLECHIN CONTROVERSY

AFTER THE S.P.R. tenancy was over one of the guests wrote a long account of his experiences at Ballechin, which was published in *The Times* on 8th June 1897. The author, Mr J. Callendar Ross (1844–1913), was a leader-writer on the staff of that newspaper, and his account was unsigned. It was printed under the caption 'On the Trail of a Ghost', which was repeated over the whole of the considerable ensuing correspondence. In his obituary it was stated that Mr Ross was a Perthshire man, from which it is reasonable to assume the possibility that he knew something of the history of Ballechin House before he went there during the S.P.R. investigation. His father was a surveyor in Perthshire, who later became the land agent to Lord Muncaster's estates at Ravenglass in Cumberland. Before joining *The Times* in 1881, Mr Callendar Ross had been a leader-writer for the *Glasgow News* and had edited the *Dumfries and Galloway Herald and Courier*. He was described as having studied medicine, as being interested in scientific subjects, and of being a writer with a 'vigorous, lucid and pungent style'.[1] He went to Ballechin in company with Sir James Crichton-Browne and Mr W. A. F. Balfour-Browne. His account of his experiences during his visit in *The Times* was highly critical of the way in which the S.P.R. investigation had been conducted.

When Mr Callendar Ross's story was published, Myers believed quite erroneously that it had been written by Sir James Crichton-Browne, F.R.S., who had been publicly critical of the S.P.R.'s methods in conducting thought-transference experiments in 1883. Sir James, in company with Sir Francis Galton, F.R.S., and George G. Romanes, F.R.S., had been invited by Professor Henry Sidgwick, the President of the S.P.R., and F. W. H. Myers to witness mental phenomena, which were claimed to be supernormal, produced by two young men, George Albert Smith (mentioned in an earlier chapter in connexion with Miss Freer's abilities in obtaining psychic messages through sea-shells) and Douglas Blackburn. Prior to the

[1] *The Times*, 14th April 1913.

'experiments' conducted by the S.P.R. leaders, Smith and Blackburn had been paid public performers in a 'second sight' act in the music-halls of Brighton. Blackburn later stated publicly in print in 1908, 1911, and 1917 that the 'experiments' were simple trickery, and that the S.P.R. investigators had been as easy to deceive as children. Sir James and his friends knew nothing of these future revelations, of course, but as a result of their own observations and some simple tests, soon became convinced that the whole thing was conjuring, as might have been expected, and said so. Sir James published a detailed account of these events in *The Westminster Gazette*, including the final clash with the infuriated Myers:

The last scene of all, or passage-at-arms, I vividly recollect. Mr Myers, standing in front of the fireplace, said: 'It must be allowed that this demonstration has been a total failure, and I attribute that to the offensive incredulity of Dr Crichton-Browne.' To which I rejoined: 'I hope I always will show offensive incredulity when I find myself in the presence of patent imposture.' [1]

Myers and the S.P.R. hushed up the affair as best they could, and suppressed all mention of the incident in the account of the experiments in their *Proceedings*, and in a privately circulated pamphlet, *Mr Blackburn's Confession*, prepared by Miss Alice Johnson, the Secretary of the Society, in 1909. This pamphlet, issued after Douglas Blackburn had published his first statement in 1908, claimed that the experiments proved telepathy and that Mr Blackburn's revelation that they were simple conjuring was not true.

Sir James's attitude to the experiments with Smith and Blackburn in 1883 still rankled with Myers in 1897. Lord Bute arranged for Sir James to visit Ballechin on the recommendation of Sir William Huggins, to which Myers could scarcely object, since Bute was paying the costs of the investigation. Myers wrote to Bute, however, on 4th April 1897:

Perhaps you will pardon me for saying privately that I don't think there will be room *for him when my little group are there! I respect his scientific attainments, but his personal manners are not encouraging to sensitives. I have seen him at it!*

When Mr Callendar Ross's account was published in *The Times* on 8th June 1897 Myers wrote to Lord Bute on the same day:

[1] For an accessible account of the incident see Sir James Crichton-Browne, M.D., LL.D., F.R.S., *The Doctor's Second Thoughts*, London, 1931. In my *The Strange Case of Edmund Gurney* the matter is fully discussed and the relevant extracts from *The Westminster Gazette* and S.P.R. literature of the period are reproduced.

1. John, 3rd Marquess of Bute, wearing St Andrews University rectorial robes.

2. Gravestone of Ada Goodrich Freer (Mrs Spoer) at Cedar Lawn Cemetery, Paterson, New Jersey, U.S.A.
Photo. Dorothy Kurtz.

3. Fr Allan McDonald.

CERTIFIED COPY OF AN ENTRY OF BIRTH

GIVEN AT THE GENERAL REGISTER OFFICE,
SOMERSET HOUSE, LONDON.

Application Number....PAS. 25496/67...........

REGISTRATION DISTRICT Uppingham

1857. BIRTH in the Sub-district of Uppingham   in the Counties of Rutland Leicester & Northampton

No.	When and where born	Name, if any	Sex	Name, and surname of father	Name, surname, and maiden surname of mother	Occupation of father	Signature, description, and residence of informant	When registered	Signature of registrar	Name entered after registration
	1	2	3	4	5	6	7	8	9	10*
107	Fifteenth May 1857 Uppingham	Ada Goodrich	Girl	George Freer	Mary Freer formerly Adcock	Veterinary Surgeon	George Freer Father Uppingham	Twenty Fifth June 1857	John Bell Registrar	

*See note overleaf.

CERTIFIED to be a true copy of an entry in the certified copy of a Register of Births in the District above mentioned.

Given at the GENERAL REGISTER OFFICE, SOMERSET HOUSE, LONDON, under the Seal of the said Office, the   6th   day of   April   1967.

BC 594944

Form A502 (S.13408) Dd.161881 30M 6/66 Hw.—RE-30

4. Miss Freer's birth certificate.

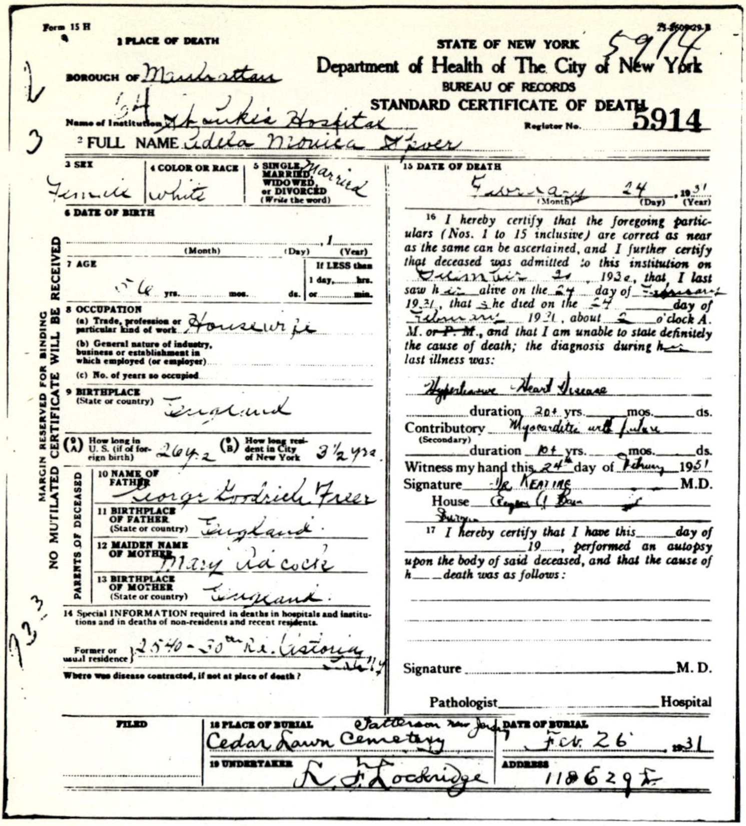

5. Miss Freer's death certificate.

I am sorry, but not much surprised, to see Crichton-Browne's letter in The Times *today, re Ballechin. That a self-invited guest should write this of his host (whose name I presume he had been desired not to mention) and his host's friends, is not alien to the conception which one brief interview with this gallant knight had given me of him. I did warn you, and I warned Miss Freer, of his* animus.

Myers' letter was wrong on both its main points. Sir James did not invite himself to Ballechin, and he did not write the letter in *The Times.* He did, however, include an account of the adventures of Mr Ross, Mr Balfour-Browne, and himself at Ballechin in his memoirs,[1] and the discussion with the driver of the wagonette that brought them from the station is too amusing to omit:

As we made our way to B., I thought it well to ask the driver if he knew what was going on there. 'Weel, sur,' he replied, 'we dinna ken, but I keep drivin' there and back queer-looking folks like you, and I thought maybe they were opening a hydropathic.' I suggested to him that perhaps they were hunting up the ghosts there, at which he laughed heartily, and said: 'Na, na! there are some Roman Catholics, but nae ghosts there; its a' havers!'

Sir James said that Miss Freer told them the story of the noises on their arrival, and regaled them with the history of the 'wicked major'. Despite this conditioning, they experienced nothing at all. 'I lay awake reading till three or four in the morning, and there was not a mouse stirring, and after that I had a tranquil sleep,' wrote Sir James, adding that, 'the breakfast party was evidently disappointed when we came down unscared and with no tale to tell.' On the second evening of their stay Miss Freer gave them some further details of the alleged manifestations:

During the Sunday evening we heard from Miss Freer and her friends further particulars of the noises, of the strange sensations by which they were frequently accompanied, to wit, rocking of the bed, tugging at the bedclothes, a sense of icy chilliness as if entering an ice-house, and of struggling with something unseen, so we went again hopefully to bed, but were again disappointed, for the silence was unbroken, and we slumbered tranquilly. We were evidently immune to ghostly visitations.'

Sir James recorded that he drew Miss Freer's attention to the peculiar construction of the house with its hollow wooden casings, its flimsy rafters, and its vibrating floors, and its situation in a

[1] Sir James Crichton-Browne, *The Doctor's After Thoughts*, London, 1932, pp. 175–84.

particularly seismic area of Scotland. Sir James confirmed in his account that the visit of Miss Chaston to Ballechin with Myers took place when Miss Freer was absent 'on an Easter visit to some friends', and that after first writing a series of letters to Bute about his experiences at Ballechin, Myers had later declined to allow their contents to be published. Sir James wrote that little need be said of the apparitions seen by Miss Freer 'at a time when she was highly strung', and that these were rather obviously 'hallucinatory in character, the offspring of suggestion upon a strongly prepossessed mind'. Sir James concluded his account:

The costly and very generously conducted experiment at B. was a fiasco—an illustration of the growth of a myth and of the magnification and misrepresentation of a few simple natural phenomena by sensitive minds in quest of the supernatural. As an old Highland woman said to Miss Freer: 'There are no ghosts at B., it was just the young callants last year that were having a lark.'

In his account in *The Times* of 8th June 1897 Mr Ross confirmed many of the points Sir James was to record in his memoirs in later years. He said that their visit to Ballechin had taken place after the enquiry 'had been going on for more than two months', *i.e.*, in May 1897 when no progress had been made. He said that the visitors were predominantly members of the S.P.R. or had sympathy with the aims of that Society, and that 'nearly all seems to have begun by assuming supernatural interference instead of leaving it for the final explanation of whatever might be clearly proved to be otherwise inexplicable'. Mr Ross gave a good deal of information about the odd construction of the house, saying that it was 'one huge sounding board transmitting and possibly intensifying certain kinds of noise'. He gave a number of examples of noises heard by him which had been traced to entirely natural origins. He told how Miss Freer was in the habit of entertaining the nervous guests at these 'haunted house parties' with stories of the ghost and its activities, and with her theory about the 'wicked major'. Mr Ross added:

The only mystery in the matter seems to be the mode in which a prosaic and ordinary dwelling was endowed with so evil a reputation. I was assured in London that it had had this reputation for 20 or 30 years. The family lawyer in Perth asserted most positively that there had never been a whisper of such a thing until the house was let for last year's shooting season to a family, whom I may call the H's.[1] I was told the

---

[1] Mr Ross was referring to the tenancy of the Heaven family in 1896. He was presumably unaware of the testimony of Fr Hayden, who had told Lord Bute of noises at Ballechin at an earlier date.

same thing in equally positive terms by the minister of the parish, a level headed man from Banffshire, who has lived in the place for 20 years. He told me that some of the younger members of the H. family had indulged in practical jokes and boasted of them. . . . The steward or factor on the estate concurs with the lawyer and minister in denying that the house had any reputation for being haunted before the advent of the H. family.

Mr Ross concluded his long article in *The Times* with a surprisingly frank criticism of Miss Freer and the S.P.R.

Lord Bute's confidence has been grossly abused by someone, and, what he will probably regret even more, he has been unwittingly led to do an appreciable injury to the owners of Ballechin. It was represented to him by someone that he was taking 'the most haunted house in Scotland', a house with an old and established reputation for mysteries if not supernatural disturbances. What he has got is a house with no reputation whatever of that kind, with no history, with nothing germane to his purpose beyond a cloud of baseless rumours produced during the last twelve months. Who is responsible for the imposture it is not my business to know or to inquire, but that it is an imposture of the most shallow and impudent kind there can be no manner of doubt. . . Without attempting to judge individuals, it must be said that an experience like the present intensifies the suspicion and disgust which close contact with the S.P.R. always tends to excite. I am well aware that among its members are many men of eminence, ability and unquestionable honesty. So on the direction of many a dubious company we find the names of men of honour and integrity. Men do not sufficiently consider the responsibility which they incur, financially or morally, when they lend the sanction of their names to proceedings which they do not control and perhaps never inquire into. Seen at all close the methods of the Society for Psychical Research are extremely repulsive. What it calls evidence is unsifted gossip, always reckless and malignant; what it calls discrimination is too often the selection from gossip, all worthless, of those portions which fit best into the theory it happens to be advocating.[1]

It is almost unnecessary to say that this article created a sensation. Miss Freer, over her pseudonym of 'Miss X', wrote at once to *The Times* to express her anger that Mr Ross, who she alleged had given an undertaking to publish nothing about Ballechin, and especially its identity, had violated her hospitality. She said that it was quite untrue to say that the name and location of the house were known in London before Mr Ross went there.[2] Unfortunately for her, this was

[1] *The Times*, 8th June 1897.   [2] *Ibid.*, 9th June 1897.

promptly contradicted in a published letter from Mrs Therese Musgrave, who wrote:

I for one can corroborate the statement made by your correspondent that the name of the house in Scotland and the names of the proposed visitors were known in London as early as March, and were spoken of without reserve.[1]

Nobody wrote in support of the assertion by Miss Freer.

The most surprising reaction to Mr Ross's letter came from F. W. H. Myers. He had stayed at Ballechin House from 12th to 22nd April 1897, during the tenancy but while Miss Freer was temporarily away from Ballechin. Myers had been enthusiastic about the phenomena after reading Miss Freer's journal. He had written to her as early as 13th March, 'It is plain that the B——case is of *great* interest. I hope we may have a discussion of it at S.P.R. general meeting, May 28th, 8.30, and perhaps July 2nd, 4 p.m., also . . . I will send back the two notebooks after showing them to the Sidgwicks. I am so very glad that you and the others have been so well repaid for your trouble.'[2] While at Ballechin Myers wrote again to Miss Freer on 15th April to discuss her proposed lecture on the case to the S.P.R., which it was agreed should be on 2nd July, but which never took place. Myers said that the noises were still going on, and that he was moving into Room No. 5 to be nearer to them. He said that he was reporting his experiences in a series of letters to Lord Bute. On 21st April he wrote again to Miss Freer in a similar vein suggesting that they should meet in London.[3] They never did, and this letter was, so far as I know, their last communication, for a reason to be discussed later. It can be said that 23rd April was the date of the personal quarrel between Miss Freer and Myers, the cause of which was, I fancy, much more human than the alleged haunting of Ballechin House and only indirectly connected with it. 8th June, when Mr Ross's letter was published, was, however, the significant date of the parting of the ways over Ballechin itself. In this incident Myers seems to have behaved very badly indeed. Whether the reason was purely fear of ridicule in the face of Mr Ross's criticisms, and the public support these received from all sides, or whether in addition the emotional upset with Miss Freer a few weeks previously was still rankling and influenced his attitude in some degree, I do not know.

[1] *The Times*, 12th June 1897.
[2] *The Alleged Haunting of B—— House*, pp. 183–4.
[3] *Ibid.*, pp. 186–7. In transcribing Myers' letters to her, Miss Freer omitted many sentences, which may have been of a personal nature.

When Mr Ross's letter appeared, Myers immediately decided that it would be expedient to disclaim Ballechin. Signing himself as Honorary Secretary of the S.P.R., he wrote to *The Times* at once and said that while he had visited Ballechin representing the Society, he had decided that there was no evidence worth reporting.[1] He did not say that he had stayed in the house for as long as ten days, accompanied by his medium Miss Chaston. He did not mention his eulogies of the case to Miss Freer. He did not reveal that he had reported his own experiences there in a series of letters to Lord Bute.[2] Nine days later he persuaded Henry Sidgwick to support him in view of the continuing public criticism. Sidgwick wrote to *The Times* to confirm that Myers had formed an 'unfavourable view' of the investigation at Ballechin, and that he and the S.P.R. Council had agreed that there was nothing worth publishing.[3] It had evidently been decided that Miss Freer should be thrown to the wolves to save the face of the Society.

Another visitor to Ballechin, signing himself 'One of the Witnesses', was highly critical of Myers' action. He wrote that from his personal knowledge he could say that Myers had testified in writing to his own experience of the phenomena, that Myers had made himself acquainted with but a very small part of the evidence, and that in repudiating the case on behalf of the S.P.R. he had not revealed his omission to place any of the evidence before the Council.[4] Miss Freer made use of this letter when defending her position in *Borderland*. She said that Myers' letter, which was lacking in both courtesy and chivalry, needed no comment from her. It was, she wrote, 'sufficiently and effectively answered by that of One of the Witnesses'.[5] Of Sidgwick's letter supporting Myers, she said that if the Council of the S.P.R. shared Myers' view, then the letter should have been written by the President, William Crookes. Sidgwick's letter was, she wrote, 'a masterpiece of saying nothing'.[6]

The next criticism of importance came from Sir James Crichton-

---

[1] *The Times*, 10th June 1897.

[2] According to Miss Freer, Myers wrote to Bute to say that his letters must 'be in no way used' (*The Alleged Haunting of B—— House*, p. 186). The private correspondence shows that Myers asked that Bute return the letters to him, which Bute did with the request that Myers should not destroy them. They were never published.

[3] *The Times*, 19th June 1897. In her letter to Lord Bute of 29th August 1897 Miss Freer said that this was not true, and that Myers had acted on his own responsibility without consulting the S.P.R. Council.

[4] *Ibid.*, 12th June 1897.

[5] *Borderland*, 1895, vol. IV, p. 307.

[6] *Ibid.*, p. 308.

Browne, who also flatly contradicted Miss Freer's allegation that the guests had agreed not to reveal the identity of the house. Sir James wrote, over the signature of 'A Late Guest at Ballechin':

In my case there was certainly no such stipulation, and had any condition of the kind been attached I should not have accepted the invitation sent to me. Science knows nothing of secrecy, which is, however, the life-blood of quackery and imposture. I went to Ballechin as an investigator on the distinct understanding that I was to assume a critical and sceptical attitude and was to have an absolutely free hand. There was, however, no call for either scepticism or criticism, as my experiences, during the two nights I spent there in one of the haunted chambers were of the most common-place description. I heard no sound of the supernatural and saw no glimmer of a ghost.[1]

Sir James said that what had struck him as so extraordinary was that even at the time of his visit, when the tenancy of Miss Freer and Colonel Taylor had been going on for so long, no attempt at experiment or research had been made. The residents and visitors, he said, 'had been sitting there all the time, agape for wonders, straining on the limits of audition, and fomenting one another's superstitions without taking any precautions to prevent deception'. He added that practical joking, hallucination, and fraud would account for the bulk of the 'phenomena', while what remained, if any, could be explained by earth tremors and by 'the creakings and reverberations of an old and somewhat curiously constructed house'. Sir James concluded his letter by observing that in regard to the Ballechin affair the S.P.R. was 'a household divided against itself', which was true.

In the same issue of *The Times* as Sir James's letter other damaging criticisms appeared. Mr John MacDonald, a former butler at Ballechin, wrote to say that he had never heard any noises for which he could not account during the whole time he lived there, and would have no hesitation in sleeping alone in the house. A correspondent signing himself 'H. R.' said that the performance of the S.P.R. at Ballechin was 'a caricature of a legal inquiry and the parody of a scientific investigation'. He added that the Society, in his view, could not have 'the remotest idea of the legal or scientific meaning and value of evidence'.[2] Two days later Mr Joseph Heaven, the previous tenant of Ballechin, wrote to *The Times* saying that he had attached no importance to the stories of the house being haunted, and that he had attributed the noises heard during his occupancy to the peculiar way in which the house was built, and to the hot-water

[1] *The Times*, 12th June 1897.   [2] *Ibid.*, 12th June 1897.

pipes. Mr Heaven said that he had no belief in ghosts.[1] His letter has already been quoted. The same day Mr Heaven's letter was published another correspondent, signing himself 'L. E. B.', wrote to say that the S.P.R.'s methods of reporting its cases brought its operations into discredit. If the Society was to invite scientific attention, said this critic, it must 'eliminate root and branch such childish methods'.[2]

The criticisms were coming thick and fast, for concurrently with the letter from Mr Heaven and 'L. E. B.' the letter from Captain J. M. S. Steuart was published, revealing his annoyance over the deceit practised on him in obtaining the tenancy, already quoted.[3] This, as we have seen, precipitated the publication of the whole of the correspondence, some half-dozen letters, between the agents for the Steuart family, Messrs R. H. Moncrieff and Co., and the agents employed by the S.P.R. representatives, Messrs T. and J. Speedy,[4] to which reference has already been made. Messrs Speedy made it clear that they had been deceived by their own clients.

18th June 1897 was an embarrassing day for the S.P.R. *The Times* published the letter from Mrs Caroline Steuart, already quoted, complaining of the deception practised upon her. Worse still, from the point of view of the exposure of Myers' part in the affair, a further letter appeared from Sir James Crichton-Browne:

Surely Mr Myers' memory is at fault when he says that he decided when at Ballechin that the evidence collected there was not of such a character as to justify its publication by the Psychical Research Society? I visited Ballechin after Mr Myers, and I was there told that he insisted on the publication of the whole transaction. I was indeed, consulted as to the propriety of including in the publication called for by Mr Myers the testimony of one witness whom there were grave grounds for discrediting.[5]

On the following day the previously quoted letter from Lord Onslow was published. This was mentioned in the discussion of the Clandon case. It was in this letter that Lord Onslow sympathized with the Steuart family and wished that 'there were some means of making this society responsible in hard cash for the effects of the light-headed nonsense by which they depreciate other people's property'.[6]

The issue of *The Times* of 21st June contained the very interesting

---

[1] *The Times*, 14th June 1897. [2] *Ibid.*, 14th June 1897.
[3] *Ibid.*, 14th June 1897. [4] *Ibid.*, 16th June 1897.
[5] *Ibid.*, 18th June 1897. It seems probable from the private correspondence that the dubious witness was Myers' friend Miss Chaston.
[6] *Ibid.*, 19th June 1897.

letter from Professor John Milne, the seismologist, which has already been discussed. On the same day appeared a letter from Dr J. A. Menzies, an old friend of the Steuart family, who said that there had been a legend of the apparition of a white lady, who used to appear once or twice a year in one of the rooms. This had been exploded by a member of the family:

His common sense told him that there must be a reason for this; and he very soon discovered that when the moon was in a certain position, her image reflected from one mirror to another bore a certain resemblance to a white figure. So that ghost was laid. I may say in conclusion, that I have stayed often in the house, and never heard any noise of the sort mentioned as ghostly; and I never heard that the house had the reputation of being haunted.[1]

Finally, on 23rd June two letters were published which some might regard as bringing down the curtain on the alleged haunting of Ballechin House. Mr C. L. A. Skinner wrote:

I have slept at Ballechin many nights during the last 20 years and in more than one room. I have spoken to eight members of my family and friends who have also passed many nights there, and not one of us has ever seen anything or heard any strange noises. I was there a fortnight in 1879, in August and September, and again in 1883, and I never even heard talks or reports of supernatural noises.

I remember the late Mr John Steuart telling me that when he succeeded to the property, he found that the house needed a good deal of repair and that, from some cause or another, the result of the repairs was to cause a good deal of reverberation in the house. The stories about the 'wicked major' are untrue. His property was left by will to his nephew, Mr John Skinner, who took the name of Steuart, and his chief eccentricity lay in keeping a number of dogs in the house.[2]

Major S. F. C. Hamilton, of the 4th Lancashire Fusiliers, wrote with military brevity:

I have slept in Ballechin, the house of my late father-in-law, hundreds of times. I have never seen or heard a ghost or had my sleep interfered with. Ballechin has been in the family since the 15th century, and it has now been left to the Research Society to discover a ghost![3]

Ballechin was summed up in a long leading article in *The Scotsman* of 18th June 1897. After an epitome of some of the most interesting

---

[1] *The Times*, 21st June 1897.
[2] *Ibid.*, 23rd June 1897.   [3] *Ibid.*, 23rd June 1897.

and amusing criticisms, the writer gave his own impression of the controversy:

The secretary of the Psychical Society, Mr Myers, wrote repudiating on behalf of the Society, all connections with the Ballechin investigations. He had been down there with a medium, whose discoveries according to a statement made by Miss X to the reporter, were of no value. One is inclined to ask if any medium's discoveries could be of any value, and how the public can be expected to give any credence to investigations which, though professedly scientific, are conducted with such assistance. At any rate, Mr Myers made up his mind that there was nothing good enough for his Society. One of the witnesses wrote challenging Mr Myers' right to arrive at any such decision, and stated that not only had he not examined the evidence on which the phenomena were supposed to rest, but he had himself personally testified in writing his experience of them. The anxiety of the secretary of the Psychical Society to clear himself of the Ballechin Ghost does not speak very well for the methods of his Society. Ill-natured people may think that if the name had not come out, he would not have been so ready to repudiate responsibility, and would have been less critical of another of these anonymous stories of anonymous ghosts which adorn the pages of the Society's Proceedings . . . If Miss X and her associates can prove that there are sounds and sights to be heard and seen at Ballechin for which it is impossible to find any natural explanation, she may earn the medal of the P.R.S., but she will have done irreparable injury to the property. A house that is said to be haunted is bad enough, but a house that is proved to be haunted by systematic observations would not be fit for habitation. If, on the other hand, she merely confirms the account given in The Times, *there may be less to complain of. But whatever effect the business may have upon the reputation and value of Ballechin, it will certainly not make the public more enamoured of the methods of these pseudo-scientific ghost hunters. A method of investigation which begins with deception and must be conducted in secrecy is not very likely to lead to truth. Even if the veil had not been drawn from the Ballechin investigations would any one have accepted a collection of anonymous testimony as being of the slightest scientific value? And the light which has been thrown by the letters in* The Times *on the manner in which these so-called investigations were conducted is not calculated to inspire confidence. It is true that they have been repudiated by Mr Myers on behalf of the Psychical Society, but no doubt Miss X and the Ballechin party would be equally ready to repudiate the results obtained by him and his medium Miss ——. The general public have never quite taken these psychical investigators at their own valuation, and now that they have fallen out among themselves it will probably think less of them still. The only person for whom it is possible to have much sympathy in connection with the business is Mr Steuart, whose property has acquired such an unfortunate notoriety owing to the doings of these ghost hunters.*

Against the background of this assembly of contemporary comment, the most recently published assessment of the case by a modern writer is of interest. On the cover of the second edition of his *Between Two Worlds* (New York, 1967) the late Dr Nandor Fodor was described as 'the most amazing psychic investigator of our time'. On pp. 222 ff., after some criticisms of *The Haunting of Borley Rectory. A Critical Survey of the Evidence* (London, 1956) and my co-authors and myself, Dr Fodor turned his attention to Ballechin:

> The only point on which I wish to take issue with Harry Price in [is?] his claim that Borley Rectory was the most haunted house in England. Nothing but the 'most' could satisfy Harry Price's narcissism. For the sake of truth I want to state that the most haunted house in England (of which Harry Price must have been well aware, from extant literature) was Ballechin House in Perthshire.

This claim for the supremacy of Ballechin over Borley by Dr Fodor, whose lack of knowledge of both cases seems to me to have been profound, was based on Miss Freer's book and some inventions of his own, including an assertion on p. 224 that the house was haunted by 'a pack of phantom dogs'. He confessed (p. 229) that when he 'wrote to the family for information whether the house is peaceful or not, [he] received a very curt non-informative answer'.

Another modern writer, Dr Alan Gauld, makes no mention of Ballechin at all in his *The Founders of Psychical Research* (London, 1968). The omission is not an isolated one, for in this account of the activities of the S.P.R. and its leaders from the first beginnings to the early 1900s the author equally makes no reference to the Burton and Clandon affairs, nor to the Scottish second sight enquiry. Dr Gauld does not comment upon the several hundred letters to Lord Bute from Myers and the other persons involved in the matters discussed in the present work, whom it might be thought are inextricably involved in any balanced account of the early history of the S.P.R.

8

MISS FREER AND THE MEDIUMS

THERE CAN be no doubt that Miss Freer was angry with F. W. H. Myers for his desertion of her during the Ballechin upheaval which started on 8th June 1897. Apart from the evidence already adduced, she went to considerable lengths to prove that Myers was not to be trusted when she published her book on Ballechin in 1899. In the centre of an otherwise blank page following the title-page she printed the following:

I visited B—— representing that Society [S.P.R.], . . . and decided that there was no such evidence as could justify us in giving the results of the inquiry a place in our Proceedings.—The Times, *10th June 1897.*

FREDERIC W. H. MYERS

Hon. Sec. *of the Society for Psychical Research*

Compare pages 189 et seq

The pages quoted showed first, by reproducing Myers' letters, that he had enthusiastically believed in the worth of Ballechin as a case of haunting, and that it was his wish that Miss Freer should lecture to the S.P.R. on the subject. Miss Freer showed that Myers had described his experiences in the house in a series of letters to Lord Bute, afterwards withdrawing this testimony. She quoted Myers' expressed pleasure that her work had been so amply rewarded. The comparison which Miss Freer invited the reader to make, in the most prominent possible position in her book, could not fail to throw the gravest doubts on Myers' honesty of purpose. She had reason for her displeasure, but it may be thought that the extreme lengths to which she went in her book to denigrate him went deeper than the Ballechin affair itself.

I believe that Miss Freer was furious with Myers from 23rd April 1897, the day she discovered that a woman friend of his, Miss Jessica Iris Chaston, described by Miss Freer as 'a "medium" ' (the sarcastic inverted commas were hers), had been a member of the party during Myers' stay at Ballechin from 12th to 22nd April. The other members of Myers' 'little group', as he termed it in his letters to Lord Bute, were 'an intimate friend' named Colin Edmund Campbell, Miss Chaston, and a woman referred to in the correspondence as 'Mrs Loof', who like Miss Chaston is mentioned nowhere in the literature of psychical research and spiritualism. She was described as Miss Chaston's attendant. In addition, Dr (later Sir) Oliver Lodge and Mrs Lodge were there, but left Ballechin before the others.

Miss Freer had temporarily absented herself from Scotland on 9th April, and did not return until 28th April. Myers had no idea that she was coming back at all, as he revealed in his letter to Bute of 23rd April, in view of the fact that the tenancy was nearing its end. On 12th April, three days after he believed Miss Freer had left the house for good, Myers arrived at Ballechin. He returned home on 22nd April, leaving Miss Chaston behind with the intention that she would stay until Monday, 26th April, in company with Mr Campbell and Mrs Loof, because the weather was especially beautiful and beneficial to her health.

It would appear that Miss Freer heard of Miss Chaston's presence at Ballechin in a letter from Lodge written on 22nd April, after his return home, and which she received the following day. On Friday, 23rd April, Miss Freer telegraphed from London to the butler at Ballechin to say that Miss Chaston, Mrs Loof, and Mr Campbell 'must leave today without fail'. The pretext for this 'peremptory notice to quit', as it was described in the correspondence, was that another visitor, Mr Macphail, was coming to Ballechin as an observer. As the house was a large one with a full staff of servants, and had accommodated sizeable groups of observers throughout the period of the Enquiry and would in fact be without guests if Myers' 'little group' left, and as Mr Macphail was not expected until the afternoon of Monday, 26th April, it may be thought that the reason given by Miss Freer for the summary ejection of Miss Chaston was not the real one. It may be thought, too, that the procedure of telegraphing instructions to the butler to dismiss Miss Chaston and the others from the house was deliberately impolite. It was stated in Myers' letters to Bute of 2nd May 1897 that 'Miss Chaston is very indignant at Miss Freer's procedure'. Saying with embarrassment that he felt he owed Bute some account of the incident, Myers added that he would 'prefer not entering upon the matter with Miss Freer',

[1] This was C. E. Campbell of Ardpatrick (1870–1951), a Fellow of Trinity Hall, Cambridge, and a member of the S.P.R. See contemporary issues of Burke's *Landed Gentry*.

which was no doubt prudent in the face of this sudden appearance of the tigress' claws.

The private correspondence shows that Sidgwick was invited to intervene, but he was not successful. The most he could ascertain from Miss Freer was a denial of any personal antagonism towards Miss Chaston. This the reader may doubt, for in her book on Ballechin Miss Freer not only violently attacked Myers, but also included some singularly unpleasant passages about Miss Chaston.

Who and what was Miss Chaston? In Miss Freer's book she is simply referred to as 'a Miss C——', and we should not have known her name, other than from the personal correspondence, if it had not been inserted in the annotated copies of *The Alleged Haunting of B—— House*. In his letter to Bute of 2nd May 1897 Myers described her as 'a middle-aged lady, head of a hospital'. Both these statements were misleading, and one is entitled to speculate on the reason for this. Jessica Iris Chaston was thirty-three, some seven years younger than Miss Freer, and was therefore hardly middle-aged. She was the proprietress of an establishment described as a small private nursing home at 36 Devonshire Street, London, which was certainly not a hospital.

If she was a medium, which was ostensibly the reason why Myers took her to Ballechin, it is remarkable that so far as I am aware her name is mentioned nowhere in the literature of spiritualism and psychical research. It is difficult to understand, moreover, why Myers selected her for the séances he wanted to hold at Ballechin. The S.P.R., and Myers in particular, were in close touch with a number of well-known mediums at this period, and it therefore seems odd that Myers should have chosen an unknown young woman for his purpose.

Was Miss Chaston even a nurse, qualified to superintend a nursing home? Doubts were raised about this at the time, and these do not seem to have been fully resolved. After her visit to Ballechin, Lord Bute seems to have been sufficiently curious to question Myers about her, and afterwards to seek the opinion of Sir James Crichton-Browne. The latter in a letter to Lord Bute of 28th May 1897 commented upon some information given by Myers about Miss Chaston's supposed antecedents. This was capable of being checked, a task to which Sir James devoted some attention.

The correspondence makes it clear that Myers had said that Miss Chaston had previously been a nurse at Chelsea Infirmary and at Addenbrookes Hospital in Cambridge. As one of the leading medical authorities in the country, Sir James was in a favourable position to ascertain whether these assertions regarding Miss Chaston's respectability had any foundation in fact. On 6th June 1897 he wrote to Lord Bute to say that he had satisfied himself that Miss Chaston was not a state registered nurse, and had never been a member of the Royal British Nursing Association. He enclosed letters from the Matrons at both Chelsea and Addenbrookes, both of whom had searched their records and declared that they had never heard of Miss Chaston. What Sir James did discover was that Miss Chaston had probably been employed for three years at Fulbourn Asylum, Cambridge.

The circumstances of Miss Chaston's subsequent career were as unusual and obscure as those surrounding her stay at Ballechin. In 1900 Jessica Iris Chaston left 36 Devonshire Street and went to live with a gentleman calling himself Earle Wellington Jenks at 38 Ashworth Mansions, Elgin Avenue, Maida Vale. In her will made on 21st April 1902 she left all her estate (amounting to about £300) to Mr Jenks. She died on 17th November 1903 at the age of thirty-nine, being described on her death certificate as Jessica Iris Trevor, the wife of Earle Wellington Jenks Trevor, although she and Mr Trevor (or Jenks, as he had previously called himself) were never married. The cause of death was mitral disease of the heart, established for several years, general oedema, which she had contracted four months previously, and acute oedema of the lungs, from which she had suffered for ten hours.

In his letter to Bute of 23rd April 1897 before the storm broke, Myers said of the visit to Ballechin, 'It so happened that both Miss Chaston and Mrs Loof were much out of health at the time and were greatly benefited by the change.' This remark does not fit very well with the comment by Miss Freer (who does not seem to have met Miss Chaston) in her book that Miss Chaston 'was described as in weak health and partially paralysed'.[1] Even if this description was true, which we are entitled to doubt, it was a singularly unkind remark to record in print. Miss Chaston was evidently not in robust health, but she was quite well enough to make the long journey from London to Perthshire. Both she and Mrs Loof 'were much out of health at the time', according to Myers, but their indisposition seems to have been such that a change of location and country air were very beneficial. Miss Chaston's later association with Mr Jenks (or Trevor), moreover, does not suggest that she was suffering from any permanent disability other than a heart condition.[2]

---

[1] *The Alleged Haunting of B—— House*, p. 185.

[2] It is odd that at least two other women with whom Myers had associations did not enjoy good health. Mrs Marshall, the wife of his first cousin, who committed suicide in 1876 after a three-year affair with Myers, was 'constantly in ill-

Miss Freer's printed comments on the psychic messages received, through Miss Chaston's alleged mediumship at Ballechin, the details of which had first been sent by Myers to Bute and then withdrawn, were sarcastic and scathing:

These remarkable disclosures included, among other details, the murder of a Roman Catholic family chaplain, at a period when the S[teuarts] were and had long been Presbyterian, the suicide of one of the family who is still living, and the throwing, by persons in mediaeval costume, of the corpse of an infant, over a bridge, which is quite new, into a stream which until lately ran underground.[1]

She remarked in print, too, that after her return to Ballechin on 28th April 1897 she enquired of the servants what had occurred during her absence. They had, she wrote, 'very definite views as to the nature and causes of the phenomena during the visit of Mr Myers' party'.[2] All this makes it clear that Miss Freer regarded Miss Chaston's mediumship, if such existed at all, as entirely fraudulent, and was prepared to say so in print in terms which seem to me to have been both malicious and defamatory.

It is of some interest in this connexion to notice that Miss Freer was also to criticize Myers bitterly in print in 1899 in her book on Ballechin over his partiality for 'the experiences of female mediums, whether hired or gratuitous', and for introducing with approval into S.P.R. *Proceedings* 'reports of spiritualist phenomena, and the lucubrations of mediums',[3] in a tirade in which the emotional overtones were very obvious.

This attack had, of course, to await the publication of *The Alleged Haunting of B—— House*, which in 1897 had not yet been written. We may notice, however, that Miss Freer found something unpleasant to say about her former friend Myers in print in *Borderland* within a few weeks of the Ballechin quarrel. In July 1897, in an article 'Psychical Research in the Victorian Era',[4] she wrote that Myers, who she coldly described as this 'important official', was imposing his influence upon the S.P.R. literature to such an extent 'that one can no longer allege that the S.P.R. is not committed to Spiritualism'. She regretted the 'loss of freshness and vigour' of the Society compared with its work in early years, and said that the

---

[1] *The Alleged Haunting of B—— House*, p. 192.   [2] *Ibid.*, pp. 199–200.
[3] *Ibid.*, p. 183.   [4] *Borderland*, 1897, vol. IV, pp. 247–53.

health' according to Dr Gauld, as was Mrs Constance Turner, who died in August 1890 at the age of twenty-five, a matter of four months after her meetings with Myers at Folkestone (*Journal*, S.P.R., June 1964, pp. 318 and 320). Miss Freer, who outlived Myers, was an exception.

present organization under the direction of Myers had 'nothing corresponding to the S.P.R. of old days', which, she said, used to publish excellent papers by a number of notable members. These she listed by name, mentioning Edmund Gurney and Professor and Mrs Sidgwick among others, but pointedly excluding Myers.

It is of additional interest to notice that within a few months of the Ballechin affair her new-found hatred of mediums spilled over into a public attack in a lecture actually delivered to an audience of spiritualists. On 17th December 1897 Miss Freer gave an address to the London Spiritualist Alliance at St James's Hall in London. The Chairman was Col G. le Mesurier Taylor, her colleague at Ballechin, who incautiously introduced her (without knowing what was to come) as 'a most acute and sympathetic observer of psychical phenomena'.[1] In her talk, which she entitled 'Hauntings', she defended the investigation of Ballechin House, which she said had been ignored by the Society for Psychical Research, despite the fact that Myers had recorded experiences during his stay there. She said that it was a matter of the deepest regret that a Society which existed for the purpose of investigation should have washed its hands of a case 'with the most complete and best authenticated record of alleged haunting which it was possible to obtain'.[2]

It was at the conclusion of her remarks that Miss Freer made her bitter observation in regard to mediums. She had previously devoted many pages of *Borderland* to a consistent support of their claims, writing, for example, in most favourable terms of the mediumship of Mrs Leonore Piper, W. Stainton Moses, and Eusapia Paladino. She was now reported as saying to an audience of members of the London Spiritualist Alliance that she strongly dissented from their practice of employing such mediums, 'a class with which she had no sympathy whatever, and for which she wished to express an entire lack of toleration'.[3]

From one who had herself been the actual medium at the Burton séances, such an outburst to a roomful of believers might be thought to be both unbecoming and most unwise. It was, moreover, a complete change in the public attitude she had maintained so consistently and successfully during many years of sitting on the fence, by displaying, on the one hand, a respectable but tolerant agnosticism

---

[1] *Light*, 1st January 1898, p. 7.   [2] *Ibid.*, 8th January 1898, p. 17.
[3] *Ibid.*, 8th January 1898, p. 17. Miss Freer had previously mildly dissociated herself from spiritualism when it suited her to do so. In her letter of 8th October 1896, printed in the *Oban Times*, she wrote of 'the superstition of spiritualism', while earlier in the same year she had denied she was a medium in a letter to the *Inverness Courier* on 8th May.

towards spiritualism, while, on the other, claiming supernatural powers of her own and acting as the paid assistant editor of an occult periodical. It may be thought, too, that this sudden and reckless abandonment, in circumstances that could hardly have been less appropriate, of her previous position in which she had obtained the best of both worlds, displayed a motivation that was almost certainly emotional in its origins. The lecture was reported in successive issues of the spiritualist periodical *Light* of 1st and 8th January 1898, accompanied by fierce criticism of Miss Freer's disparagement of mediums. The leading article of 1st January was wholly devoted to this, accompanied by the publication of hostile and sarcastic correspondence, but this did not prevent Miss Freer from returning unrepentant to the attack as soon as an opportunity publicly to do so presented itself.

On 5th December 1898 Frank Podmore, the Joint Honorary Secretary of the S.P.R., gave an address to the Sesame Club in London on the Society's experiments with the medium Mrs Leonore Piper.[1] Miss Freer rose to speak during the discussion and was reported as saying:

She had known many mediums, and she had disliked them all. They were emotionally flabby, coarse and irreverent, much given to inflict upon you morality of the copy-book order.

She then extended her criticism to include the S.P.R. (and, of course, Myers) for experimenting with Mrs Piper, causing pain and suffering to the wretched medium. She was reported as actually saying:

Her strongest reason for objecting to the Piper experiments was the gross brutality of the whole thing. Had they a right to subject a fellow-creature to such convulsions—apparently epileptic fits—as Mrs Piper exhibited in her trances, even for the purpose of scientific discovery? She had had Mrs Piper at her feet in tears, begging to be saved from the kind of life she was leading.[2]

It is hardly necessary to say that this outburst created an uproar.

Mrs Bessie Russell-Davies made a spirited and caustic reply to Miss Freer's attack on mediums. She (Mrs Davies) was a Spiritualist, and not only a Spiritualist, but one of those vulgar and degraded mediums.[3]

The controversy thus started by Miss Freer continued for many

[1] 'Parleying with Spirits', *Light*, 17th December 1898, pp. 612–13.
[2] *Light*, 17th December 1898, p. 613.   [3] *Ibid.*, p. 613.

weeks in the pages of *Light*. Dr Richard Hodgson of the S.P.R. wrote that Mrs Piper 'was indignant at Miss Freer's remarks as reported in *Light*'. He said that no such incident between Mrs Piper and Miss Freer, as described by the latter, had ever occurred, and that Mrs Piper had never suffered at the hands of the S.P.R. He inferred that there had been little personal contact between the two ladies at all, and that 'the starting point for Miss Freer's mis-representations' was probably an occasion when both had been in Cambridge and had been walking through the College grounds (presumably Trinity) with Myers and a friend, who had momentarily walked on in front leaving Mrs Piper and Miss Freer together. Hodgson quoted from a letter written to him by Mrs Piper on 5th January 1899 after the incident at the Sesame Club, in which the medium said that she had never suffered pain during her trances, and had never told anybody, including Miss Freer, that she did.[1]

In her reply, published a week later,[2] Miss Freer said that it was Dr A. T. Myers[3] of the S.P.R., the brother of F. W. H. Myers, who had asked her to visit Mrs Piper in London, 'where, not at Cambridge, the incidents to which I have referred took place'. As for Mrs Piper's denials that she had suffered 'gross brutality' at the hands of the S.P.R., Miss Freer wrote, 'It does not surprise me that Mrs Piper's memory should appear to be affected by her experiences.'

At the end of her reply Miss Freer declared that as regards the remarks attributed to her at the Sesame Club, she could not hold herself responsible for a newspaper report of anything she said. The room was crowded, she wrote, and hearing was difficult. This was instantly seized upon by her critics. A correspondent wrote to say that he had been sitting close to Miss Freer and 'heard all too plainly the words which fell from her lips. They do not look pretty in print, but Miss Freer must take their entire responsibility.'[4] The Editor added that the report in *Light* was perfectly accurate.[5] This giving of the lie to Miss Freer was supported by Mrs Bessie Russell-

---

[1] 'Miss Freer and Mrs Piper', *Light*, 4th February 1899, pp. 55–6.

[2] *Ibid.*, *Light*, 11th February 1899, p. 67.

[3] As the reader knows, it was not Miss Freer's habit to reveal the actual names of the witnesses she claimed were involved in her stories. The example of her friend 'the Hon. Mrs G., now abroad', who she declared could corroborate her account of the Burton sittings, will be recalled. She was safe, however, in the case of Dr A. T. Myers, who had died of a self-administered overdose of narcotics on 10th January 1894, five years previously (*The Strange Case of Edmund Gurney*, pp. 12, 16, and 199).

[4] 'Miss Goodrich-Freer and Mrs Piper', *Light*, 18th February 1899, p. 83.

[5] *Ibid.*, p. 83.

Davies, who wrote to say that she had been present at the Sesame Club, and assured her readers that all that Miss Freer 'had to say in regard to Mrs Piper, and her abuse of other mediums, was very distinctly heard by myself and your very trustworthy reporter, who sat on the chair next to me, and I made it my business to ask him if he heard distinctly'. Mrs Davies concluded her remarks by saying:

I know her [Miss Freer] personally, and believe her to be distinctly incapable of forming a reliable opinion on psychic subjects from her own observation—what she may have read or gleaned from others' experience does not count for anything. Her patronising pity for 'poor Mrs Piper' is wasted, and I cannot help feeling sorry for her when I see that she has to resort to throwing doubts on your reporter to escape the consequences of her attack on Mrs Piper, Spiritualism, and 'all mediums'. I very much regret that 'all mediums' were not present to hear her opinion of them; if they had been I fancy she would in future have to depend entirely on her own 'mediumship' for something to talk about, and the result would then be very small indeed.[1]

The dispute spread to America. Miss Lilian Whiting of the American branch of the S.P.R., writing from Boston, Mass., said:

It is amazing to all those who are familiar with the trance phenomena exhibited through Mrs Piper, and with the earnest, sincere, and most faithful and enlightened work of Dr Hodgson, in the patient investigation of years, that any intelligent person can make the singularly reckless statements regarding Mrs Piper that appear over the signature of Miss Freer.[2]

The year 1899 marked a climacteric in Miss Freer's career, and no doubt she took stock of her position. The Ballechin quarrel with Myers and her emotional reaction to it had lost her at one stroke the sympathy of both the spiritualists and the S.P.R., the two main classes of credulous persons upon whom she had relied over the years for part of her living and her literary ambitions. She had deserted her benefactor W. T. Stead in favour of Lord Bute, and *Borderland* had ceased publication two years before. Her comfortable home with her friend Constance Moore's family, with whom she had first lived at Holy Trinity Vicarage, Paddington, and later at 27 Cleveland Gardens,[3] had ceased, and Miss Freer and Miss Moore had set up

[1] 'Mrs Piper and Miss Goodrich-Freer', *Light*, 25th February 1899, p. 95.
[2] 'Miss Goodrich-Freer and Mrs Piper', *Light*, 11th March 1899, p. 112.
[3] Although Miss Freer was only a guest at 27 Cleveland Gardens, she invariably referred to this address as 'my London house' in her letters to Lord Bute.

house together at The Laurels, Bushey Heath. In April 1899 Miss Freer and Miss Moore had relinquished their part-time appointments at Swanley Horticultural College, following a difference of view with the governing body. On 31st July Miss Freer wrote to Lord Bute that she had 'lately given away a psychic library', presumably her own, suggesting that her interest in the subject was ending.

On the other hand, Miss Freer had the invaluable folklore material she had obtained from Fr Allan McDonald during the second sight expeditions to the Highlands and the Isles in previous years, of which she was already making free use in her career as a writer and lecturer. Preparations for what was ultimately to be virtually a complete change from psychical research to folklore as the subject for her literary work had already begun concurrently with her first attacks on Myers and the mediums in July and November 1897. From the last months of 1897 to her departure from England at the end of 1901 she was to lecture on Hebridean folklore and history to the Viking Club, the Folklore Society, the Scottish Society of Literature and Art, the Gaelic Society of Glasgow, and similar institutions, and articles over her name on these subjects were published in *The Contemporary Review*, *Blackwood's Edinburgh Magazine* and other journals of the period.

The other important advantage she still enjoyed in 1899 was the continued patronage of Lord Bute, who took the side of Miss Freer in the quarrel with Myers and the S.P.R., and it was his help that enabled her to publish her book on the case in 1899 with his name on the title-page as co-author. Unfortunately for her, Lord Bute was to suffer his first apoplectic attack in August 1899, to be followed by a second seizure on 8th October 1900, to which he succumbed the next day without rallying.

Miss Freer's first book, *Essays in Psychical Research*, a collection of material previously published in periodicals, appeared in May 1899. It was scathingly reviewed by Dr Richard Hodgson of the S.P.R.[1] Hodgson said the book dealt with its subject in the popular manner of *Borderland* rather than in any scientific way, which would reduce its value and interest for many readers. He complained that in her essay on the divining rod she had used material of Sir William Barrett, previously in S.P.R. *Proceedings*, without acknowledgment. But Hodgson had most to say about Miss Freer's 'misrepresentation of fact' regarding Mrs Piper, and brought out again the whole of the controversy in *Light*. The reviewer implied, with perfect truth and

---

[1] *Proceedings*, S.P.R., 1899, vol. XIV, pp. 393–6.

possibly with inside knowledge, that on the subject of mediums Miss Freer's views were emotional and obsessional.

Miss Freer is evidently labouring under an idée fixe, *which perhaps began between two and three years ago, and has become more strongly established since.*

In my opinion Dr Hodgson's dating of the beginning of Miss Freer's obsession in regard to mediums is correct, in that it commenced at the time of the quarrel with Myers over Miss Chaston in the spring of 1897.

A few weeks later *The Alleged Haunting of B—— House* was published. The S.P.R. review by Frank Podmore[1] was seriously critical, as could have been expected. Podmore said that Miss Freer's 'laborious journal' of her stay in the house was 'quite unimpressive', although conceding that if experiments in other allegedly haunted houses had been described in a similar way 'they might be found to make even duller reading'. The reviewer complained that no attempt had been made to ascertain the source of the sounds, or 'even to have determined whether or not the sounds which they described day after day were objective'. Podmore added:

But, after all, the main reason why the recital of these various manifestations fails to impress us has still to be told. It was Miss Freer who first saw a ghostly figure; it was again Miss Freer who first heard ghostly noises, and throughout these records it is Miss Freer who is most frequently and most conspicuously favoured with 'phenomena'. Miss Freer has shown that she knows how to observe clearly and how to record accurately, but, for all that, her testimony in a matter of this kind carries very little weight.

Podmore, after commenting upon Miss Freer's unusual liability to hallucinations, although conceding that she was 'not of course responsible for this mental idiosyncrasy', said that it must seriously impair the value of her testimony. He thought that the apparition of the nun Ishbel 'had her birth in the percipient's imagination'. Podmore said that of the remainder of the odds and ends of reported phenomena 'it is hardly necessary to speak'. It is odd that nowhere in the review did Podmore mention the name of Miss Freer's co-author, Lord Bute.

[1] *Proceedings*, S.P.R., 1900, vol. XV, pp. 98–100.

9

MISS FREER, SWANLEY, AND THE LAST YEARS

DURING HER last years in England Miss Freer maintained a correspondence with Fr Allan McDonald, most of which has unfortunately been destroyed. His diary, however, kept from September 1897 to June 1898, shows that it was extensive. One of her objects seems to have been to obtain his help in translations from Gaelic, a language with which she was not familiar, for her purpose in making use of his folklore material over her own name. From his side there seems to be little doubt that Fr Allan had 'fallen' rather badly for Miss Freer, as most men she met seemed to do in one way or another. A sentimental attachment of this kind, entirely innocent in its nature, would be quite normal in Fr Allan's circumstances. He was living in isolation and celibacy and was not in good health, and to have an attractive and intelligent woman arrive in Eriskay and tell him that his folklore collection was of scientific value and encourage him to collect more would mean a very great deal to him. It seems fairly obvious, however, from his diary entries that his emotions were involved. If an expected letter from Miss Freer did not arrive, he was acutely disappointed and entered the fact in his diary. He wrote that his friendship with Miss Freer had been 'an education of mind and soul, and has thrown sunshine over the last two years of my life'. In his diary he called her sometimes the 'lady of the ghosts', but more often simply 'the little lady'. He wrote, 'The more I know of Miss Freer the holier she seems. May God ever guide her and have her in His keeping.' Miss Freer does not seem to have returned this affectionate regard, for on occasions Fr Allan noted ruefully in his diary that she sometimes even confused him with Fr MacDougall, the parish priest of Benbecula, and that letters from her went astray in consequence. But there can be no doubt that she kept Fr Allan's nose to the grindstone in connexion with the work that she invited him to do, and that Fr Allan willingly followed her instructions. His diary records *inter alia* that he spent many hours answering lists of questions sent to him, gathering information which she required for papers and lectures, lending her his MSS., and translating material for her that had been written in Gaelic.

A few surviving letters from Miss Freer to Fr Allan McDonald throw some light on her life at this period. She and Miss Constance Moore were still living together at The Laurels, Bushey Heath, in 1900, the year in which Miss Freer's book on Ballechin House had evidently been sufficiently successful to justify a second and revised edition. Despite this, there seem to have been financial difficulties. As Lady Margaret Macrae wrote in a letter already quoted, Lord Bute died in 1900 and his help ceased in that year. Doubtless to her surprise and disappointment, Miss Freer was not mentioned in Lord Bute's will. Miss Moore had to take a job in London to make ends meet. 'Alas! I am tied to work in town now, and only get week-ends of holiday,' she wrote to Fr Allan in June in response to his suggestion that she might revisit the Hebrides.[1] The two friends were looking for a smaller house ('the object of moving is economy,' wrote Miss Freer to Fr Allan in October), but without success.

Miss Freer had suffered a severe breakdown during the winter of 1900–1, and 'was very ill for some months' as she wrote to Fr Allan on 28th August 1901. One wonders what was the cause of this collapse on the part of a woman who had always boasted of her exceptional health and vigour. 'I am *so tired*,' she wrote in the same letter to Fr Allan. She had, of course, expended much energy in the preceding years in writing, lecturing, ghost-hunting, touring the Highlands and the Isles, and in public controversy. On the other hand, she was only forty-four, and was still sufficiently youthful in appearance to pass as at least ten years less than her real age.[2] The breakdown was, moreover, a temporary one despite its evident severity, as was demonstrated by the active life of travel and literary activity she was soon to resume.

If one looks for some special cause for Miss Freer's breakdown at this time, it is reasonable to recall that F. W. H. Myers died on 17th January 1901. On the assumption that there had been a relationship between Myers and Miss Freer from the days of her introduction

[1] Miss Moore's letters to Fr Allan, her only personal papers I have seen, suggest that she was a very sincere, sympathetic, and rather colourless person, completely dominated by Miss Freer. It is interesting that she never joined the S.P.R., despite her companionship with Miss Freer over many years, including the expeditions to the Hebrides and the stay at Ballechin. The reason is presumably that stated by Miss Freer in her letter to Bute of 25th January 1896 in which she said that Miss Moore 'scorns the whole subject' of psychical research.

[2] Four years after Myers' death Miss Freer married Dr H. H. Spoer, who was sixteen years her junior yet who seems to have believed that his wife was about his own age.

to the S.P.R., then the death of possibly the first man in her life could have been a sufficiently severe shock to precipitate her illness. Her emotional attacks upon him after the Ballechin quarrel over Miss Chaston would, I fancy, support this view rather than the reverse, as would the coincidence of her breakdown with the time of Myers' last illness and death and a remark in her letter to Fr Allan McDonald that if it were not for Miss Moore she would seriously consider retiring into a convent.

Another mystery connected with Miss Freer's health, and possibly her sex life, at this precise period, is contained in a single letter passing between two ladies who knew her well, and who shall be nameless. The letter is dated 28th February 1901, six weeks after Myers' death.

She [Miss Freer] talks of coming to live in London, and asked me if I would go and 'stroke' her sometimes as it does her good. I don't think that can all be flattery, because she couldn't stand it if it didn't do her some good, but on the other hand she must know I should enjoy immensely doing anything of the sort.

Dr Campbell is of the opinion that this letter means that Miss Freer wanted her friend to soothe and flatter her during this period of disturbed health and low spirits. Dr E. J. Dingwall, on the other hand, takes the view that Miss Freer was seeking the pleasures of flagellation, as demonstrated by the suggestion that the experience would be one Miss Freer would find difficulty in enduring but for the benefit it brought her, and that her partner in what was proposed would herself obtain immense enjoyment from beating Miss Freer. The word 'stroke', placed in quotation marks by the writer of the letter, would lend itself to either interpretation.

Whatever the answers to these questions may be, it is clear that in the early months of 1901 Miss Freer was not her usual self, and had been through a period of ill-health and mental depression. The point is a not unimportant one, because there seems to be no doubt that during the summer of 1901 something occurred that irretrievably damaged Miss Freer's reputation as a psychical researcher and clairvoyante. There is some evidence to show that she was detected in fraud for the first time since the commencement of her career in the late 1880s. She had previously avoided exposure over this long period by shrewdly confining her activities to crystal-gazing, shell-hearing, clairvoyance, the seeing of apparitions, and so forth, all of which relied entirely upon her own plausibility and the avoidance, as we have seen, of any investigation of her stories by the consistent concealment of names and locations in her accounts. An explanation of her downfall at this time could be that her normal extreme caution had been impaired by ill-health.

I believe that the incident, the occurrence of which has been concealed until now, took place shortly before 13th August 1901. On that day Alexander Carmichael, who had spoken in earlier days in such glowing terms of Miss Freer, wrote cautiously to Fr Allan that he thought it right to tell him that news had reached him from London 'that Miss Freer is not altogether what she seems, and draws upon her imagination a good deal for her facts. I deem it right to tell you this much, my dear friend'. It may be thought that it would be a considerable embarrassment to Carmichael to make even this small preliminary disclosure to a close friend in the far-away Hebrides, for he knew that Fr Allan had an affectionate and high regard for Miss Freer, an opinion that Carmichael had previously shared with enthusiasm. But Carmichael was a conscientious person, no doubt concerned, in the light of what was being whispered in London, at the influence he knew Miss Freer could exert over the unsuspecting Fr Allan in distant Eriskay. 'I fear', wrote Carmichael to Fr Allan, 'that I think less of Miss Freer than I did.' Having broken the ice, Carmichael followed the matter up with a more positive statement in a further letter to Fr Allan on 7th October 1901.

We hear from various sources that Miss Freer is not genuine and some call her a clever imposter. I never got my wife to believe in her. In London it is said that one society after another, and one man after another, have thrown her off.

Finally, on 25th March 1902, Carmichael made specific reference to the incident and disclosed in his letter to Fr Allan that it had occurred in the village of Swanley in Kent, where 'they turned upon her for her lies, pretence and imposture', and Miss Freer 'had to clear out'. Most unfortunately, Carmichael gave no other details or identification of the occurrence, merely adding, 'Quite a number of her friends in London have found her out and will not have anything to do with her'. It seemed probable from this, but not certain, that this ostracism stemmed from the Swanley exposure.

The suggestion that Carmichael's letters constituted a developing account of the embarrassing discovery of Miss Freer in fraud is possibly confirmed by her own letter to Fr Allan already quoted of 28th August 1901. This was written a matter of only two weeks after the first letter from Carmichael. It clearly referred to some recent disturbing episode, for she apologized for not writing for so long, and gave as the reason that she had experienced 'much anxiety and uncertainty about various matters'. She said, moreover, that Mrs Jenner, the wife of Henry Jenner of the British Museum, the authority on the old Cornish language and a near neighbour at Bushey Heath, was saying that Miss Freer and Miss Constance Moore had quarrelled after living together for twenty-one years. The truth of the matter, explained Miss Freer, who did not deny the fact of the parting, was that Miss Moore had had 'severe family troubles', that it was now 'necessary for her to be much in London', and that it would be better for her to be 'among her relatives which is what *they* want'. Miss Freer said that she and Miss Moore were disposing of The Laurels, for which they had received a satisfactory offer,[1] and Miss Freer was accepting an invitation to visit the Holy Land.

What was the incident at Swanley? For some time I thought that it might be connected with Miss Freer's resignation of her post as a joint secretary, with Miss Moore, of the women's branch of the Swanley Horticultural College in April 1899, but I now think this improbable for four reasons. First, the resignation had taken place over two years before Carmichael's letters to Fr Allan on the subject of the downfall of Miss Freer at Swanley, the whole tone of which suggested a recent occurrence. Secondly, the notion that Miss Freer had been discovered in lies, pretence, and especially *imposture*, in carrying out her prosaic part-time duties on the secretarial staff of a horticultural college, seemed divorced from reality. Thirdly, Miss Moore also resigned on the same date from her similar position, which indicates that the reason was one which concerned both joint secretaries, who could scarcely have both been detected in imposture and lies. Finally, Carmichael's quotation of the expressed opinions that Miss Freer was 'not genuine' and was 'a clever imposter', and his reference to her consequent ostracism by her friends in London, point clearly, or so it seems to me, to Miss Freer's activities in psychical research, a subject in which imposture and lack of genuineness are unfortunately exceedingly common.

It follows that I believe that the Swanley location was coincidental, and that the disaster that overtook Miss Freer in that village in the summer of 1901 had nothing to do with her appointment at the horticultural college in earlier years. If this is accepted, then it can be said at once that the hypothesis that Miss Freer was exposed as a fraud in psychical research activities at Swanley would offer a more adequate explanation than that given by Miss Freer for the parting

[1] An attempt to discover whether The Laurels was jointly owned by Miss Freer and Miss Moore or, as seems more probable, was the sole property of Miss Moore, has not been successful.

with Miss Moore. It would account for Miss Freer's decision to leave England and the cessation of her membership of the S.P.R., and would provide a reason for the disappearance of all the files dealing with her affairs from the Society's archives. It would explain the suppression of all approving references to her in the publication of Sidgwick's 'Journal' in *Henry Sidgwick. A Memoir* five years later, and the surprising fact that after 1901 Miss Freer's name was scarcely ever mentioned again in S.P.R. literature, despite her large and enthusiastically praised contributions to the early volumes of *Proceedings*.

I told Dr Campbell, when he posed the problem of Swanley in his first letter to me, that there was no mention of any such incident in the entire published literature of psychical research so far as I was aware, and that an investigation of such a postulated event of over sixty years ago, mentioned only once and without details in private correspondence of the period, might well present insuperable difficulties. It was a sobering thought that our knowledge of the matter was limited to the occurrence of the presumed incident in the small village of Swanley during the summer of 1901, although it was a reasonable inference from the disappearance of the S.P.R. files that the Society was involved, and had hushed the matter up because of Miss Freer's prominence in that organization. These were the only slender leads we possessed.

An examination of the published work of the S.P.R. leaders at this period produced one very interesting clue. In 1902 Frank Podmore's book *Modern Spiritualism* appeared. To his discussion of the mediumship of Mrs Leonore Piper in the second volume he had added a footnote, presumably at a late stage in the preparation of the MS.

So far as I am aware, no other clairvoyant medium of note since 1848 has failed at one time or another to exhibit physical phenomena, if only to the extent of table-rapping, as part of her mediumistic gifts.[1]

Podmore added that sometimes these physical phenomena, which, according to him, *all* clairvoyant mediums except Mrs Piper had exhibited, 'have not been made public at all'. It seems to me that the addition of this footnote by Podmore, buried though it is in a book of nearly seven hundred pages, is of the highest importance in connexion with the mystery before us. Miss Freer had been one of the most prominent clairvoyantes ever associated with the S.P.R. in its early years, sponsored by Myers and enthusiastically commended by Sidgwick, Crookes, and others. Podmore knew her well, and it

[1] *Modern Spiritualism*, London, 1902, vol. II, p. 332, n. i.

is impossible to believe that he had forgotten about her when he wrote this footnote. Yet Podmore, having just completed *Modern Spiritualism*, the most complete survey of the subject ever attempted either then or now, was the one man who knew better than anyone else that there was *nothing in the published literature* that even hinted that Miss Freer had ever departed from her chosen and safe field of clairvoyance, visions, telepathy, shell-hearing, and the like. We may therefore think, on the basis of this footnote, that Podmore had become privately aware, some time shortly before 1902, that Miss Freer had indulged in table-rapping, the crudest of all forms of fraudulent spiritualist phenomena, or had exhibited some other alleged manifestations of the séance room. Was this the postulated incident at Swanley? It can at least be said that the dates coincide, and it may also be thought that if Miss Freer did try her hand at table-rapping without the advantage of experience, at a time when her physical and mental health was not good, these could well be the circumstances in which she was at long last caught out in trickery.

Carrying the argument further, it may be thought that the inner circle of the S.P.R. would be aghast at the discovery of Miss Freer in fraud. Previous disasters, like the enforced printed withdrawals in *Proceedings* of the ludicrous stories of Sir Edmund Hornby and 'Mr X.Z.', the exposures of the Society's pet mediums Miss Wood and Miss Fairlamb, the confession of trickery by the 'mind-reading' Creery sisters, the suicide of Edmund Gurney in 1888,[1] and the subsequent upheavals over Clandon and Ballechin, had made the S.P.R. sensitive and vulnerable over any further embarrassment in connexion with its published work. The panicking by Myers and Sidgwick and the immediate desertion of Miss Freer in the face of the first criticism of Ballechin had been entirely symptomatic of this anxiety. It is obvious, moreover, that the silence over Swanley, the obliteration of Miss Freer's name from the S.P.R. literature after 1901, the disappearance of all the files of matters with which she had been concerned, and the suppression of Sidgwick's early praise of her qualities are facts which must have *some* explanation.

All this pointed in one direction, and that was to Swanley. The theory now to be put to the test envisaged that there was in Swanley a house in which Miss Freer had been caught in fraudulently producing physical phenomena, of which Podmore had specifically mentioned table-rapping, and that as a result Miss Freer had been forced to 'clear out'. The circumstances also suggested the possibility that it was from Miss Freer's disillusioned host that Podmore received the private information on which his guarded footnote was

[1] These affairs are discussed in my *The Strange Case of Edmund Gurney*.

based. Since, however, the S.P.R. was able to keep the matter secret to some extent, an additional inference might be that the unknown person in Swanley, despite his or her annoyance, had reason not to be anxious to have the matter noised abroad. It seemed increasingly clear that we were looking for someone in Swanley who knew both Miss Freer and Podmore, and membership of the S.P.R. seemed the most obvious connexion between them and the postulated unknown person. The List of Members of the S.P.R. dated February 1901 was consulted and showed only one name in Swanley, the Rev. Charles J. M. Shaw, living at a house called The Orchard. This discovery was of extreme interest, for it will be recalled that the annotated copies of *The Alleged Haunting of B——* reveal that the Rev. Shaw had been one of Miss Freer's visitors at Ballechin House; he had also been a member of one of her *Borderland* spiritualist circles. According to John Ritchie Findlay Mr Shaw had 'a thorough belief in the supernatural'.

The Rev. Shaw's connexion with Podmore was of equal interest. At some time prior to May 1900 Mr Shaw had invited a professional medium, Alfred Peters, to be his guest at The Orchard, where demonstrations of clairvoyance were given. A second visit to The Orchard was paid by Peters in May 1900 for further clairvoyance, which was however followed by an exhibition of physical phenomena, this having been forecast by Mr Peters' 'Hindu control' at the séances.

The Rev. Shaw decided that as an S.P.R. member he should give an account of these sittings, which had greatly impressed him, to the Society. He evidently thought that Frank Podmore was the appropriate person to whom the story should be told. Podmore recorded that Mr Shaw first gave him a verbal account of the sittings with Peters in November 1900 and later sent him a detailed written statement on 6th February 1901. This was published by the S.P.R. with an introductory note by Podmore in July 1901.[1] Podmore repeated the story in *Modern Spiritualism* (vol. II, pp. 259–62) without, however, revealing that the séances took place at Swanley, so that this place-name does not appear in the book or its index. The account was mainly devoted to the physical phenomena exhibited by Peters.

In July 1901 Miss Freer was without a patron, and on the evidence of her correspondence with Fr Allan McDonald was short of money at the time. In July 1901 Miss Freer would learn from her

---

[1] *Journal*, S.P.R., July 1901, pp. 104–9. In his account Mr Shaw made it clear that he had 'engaged the services' of the medium, from which it is proper to conclude that Peters was paid a fee.

S.P.R. *Journal* that the Rev. C. J. M. Shaw, her supporter at Ballechin and a member of one of her Borderland spiritualist circles,
had twice hospitably entertained a professional medium as a guest at
his home and had been much impressed by the phenomena he had
seen.

Miss Freer would also know, having been acquainted with the
Rev. Shaw since the Ballechin affair in 1897, that he was no ordinary
vicar. She had described him, indeed, four years earlier in her letter
to Lord Bute of 17th March 1897, as a man of means and position.
He was a member of the great Kentish family of Shaw of Eltham,
and became the eighth Baronet in 1909. He had married Elizabeth
Louisa Whatman Bosanquet, the daughter of J. E. Bosanquet of
Pennenden and Claysmore, and of Lombard Street. To Miss Freer,
who had lost the patronage of Lord Bute by his death in the previous year, Mr Shaw might well seem to be a useful person to be
cultivated by an early visit to The Orchard at Swanley.

All this was, of course, an elaborate inference from the few facts
available. I suggested to Dr Campbell that the theory could be confirmed or otherwise by an approach to the ninth Baronet, Sir John
Best-Shaw, to enquire whether he knew that a Miss Freer did in
fact visit his father at The Orchard, Swanley, in 1901. If that was
established, then it might be thought that the Swanley mystery was
explained.

Dr Campbell accepted my suggestion and has both visited and
corresponded with Sir John, who was born in 1895 and was therefore a boy of six in 1901. His evidence has been given most con-
scientiously, and is strictly limited to his positive recollections. It
amounts to the following:

*1. Sir John remembers Miss Freer coming to stay with his parents
at The Orchard in 1901. He cannot recall the season of the year.*
*2. He remembers that his mother told him long afterwards that Miss
Freer was the author of the book on Ballechin House, which his
father had visited.*
*3. He remembers that his mother told him that his father had detected
'a lady' faking table-rapping at a séance somewhere. He cannot positively recall that his mother said that it was Miss Freer although he
can say that no other name was mentioned.*

The reader may think that it is of some interest that although Sir
Charles Shaw remained a member of the S.P.R. until his death in
1922, no further accounts of psychical phenomena from his pen were
contributed to the Society's literature after July 1901. It may be
thought, too, that as it was Frank Podmore to whom Sir Charles

first gave his verbal account of Alfred Peters' phenomena in November 1900, and it was again to Podmore that Sir Charles sent his written statement in February 1901, it would be to Podmore that Sir Charles would confide the story of what Miss Freer had done at Swanley. Sir Charles's position would be an embarrassing one. He had supported Miss Freer's accounts of her experiences at Ballechin, and had allowed his testimony to be printed in the book published only two years previously. He knew now that she was a fraud. From his point of view he would doubtless wish for as little publicity as possible. On the other hand, as a conscientious man, he doubtless felt that he had a duty to inform a leading member of the Society for Psychical Research. Podmore was the obvious choice. This would fully explain the discreet footnote added to p. 332 of the second volume of Podmore's *Modern Spiritualism*, which was to be published in the following year.

For obvious reasons Podmore would have to inform the Society's Council of what had happened. For one thing, in her books published only two years previously Miss Freer had claimed to be a member of several S.P.R. committees and to be an official of the Society. Whatever the truth of these statements may have been, she was certainly no longer a member of any of the four committees of the Society by the time she left England in December 1901,[1] and not long afterwards her connexion with the Society ceased altogether, despite her claim to be a member to the end of her life.

It can hardly be doubted that in the nature of things the story would have leaked out to some extent[2] by the late summer of 1901, and it seems significant that Carmichael told Fr Allan in the first two of his three letters about Miss Freer that his information came from London, where the S.P.R. had its headquarters. 'In London it is said that one Society after another and one man after another have thrown her off', wrote Carmichael in October 1901.

[1] *Journal*, S.P.R., March 1902, pp. 195-7.
[2] The S.P.R. has always had its gossips. It will be recalled, for example, that after the opening of F. W. H. Myers' sealed 'posthumous message' on 13th December 1904, for comparison with the hoped-for divination of its contents in the automatic writings of Mrs A. W. Verrall, the matter was reported in the national Press. Sir Oliver Lodge, after opening the sealed message before a selected audience, lugubriously conceded that the 'experiment has completely failed, and it cannot be denied that the failure is disappointing'. The 'leaking' of this disaster to the Press was regarded with severe displeasure by the S.P.R. leaders. 'It has become necessary to reiterate this caution,' it was stated, 'because a flagrant violation of the rule has recently occurred in the unauthorised communication to the public press of the essential part of a statement that appeared in the *Journal* for January' (*Journal*, S.P.R., January 1905, p. 13, and February 1905, p. 32).

The subsequent career of Miss Freer is not a matter for detailed discussion here. In December 1901, a few months after the Swanley episode, she left England to live in Jerusalem, and it was there that she wrote the preface to her *Outer Isles* in May 1902. Her *Inner Jerusalem* was published in 1904. The break with psychical research and her former life and interests in England was complete.[1]

In her letter of 28th August 1901 to Fr Allan McDonald, Miss Freer said she had received an invitation to visit the Holy Land for a year. As might have been expected, she refrained from giving any other information, but it is reasonable to suppose that among Miss Freer's circle this suggestion could scarcely have come other than from the widowed Marchioness of Bute and her family. They were property owners in Jerusalem, and had fulfilled the late Marquess's instructions to bury his heart on the Mount of Olives in the early winter of 1900. Later correspondence in the Bute family papers indicates in fact that Miss Freer was employed by the Butes as their agent in Jerusalem, and that in the event she did not revisit England for nearly ten years.

It is possible that despite lack of belief in Miss Freer's alleged powers as a clairvoyante, *etc.*, the Butes may have felt some sense of obligation towards her as a friend of the late Marquess. If it be assumed that the family had been informed of the Swanley affair, however, an alternative and more likely possibility is that Miss Freer's departure from England at this time, if it could be arranged, would not be unwelcome to them. They would be acutely conscious that her name had been prominently associated with that of their late father in psychical research matters. Although Swanley, with its embarrassments for both the S.P.R. and the Rev. Charles Shaw, had received no publicity, there was no guarantee that this situation would necessarily continue. An offer of paid employment far away from England at this special time seems a considerable coincidence if it was not connected with Swanley.

Miss Freer continued to live in Jerusalem, and in 1905 married there a German–American, Hans Henry Spoer, an authority on the language of the Near East. We have no information regarding her conjugal relations with her husband, but the difference of sixteen years in their ages must have made it no ordinary union, despite Dr Spoer's apparent belief that his wife was about the same age as himself.

Miss Freer's *In a Syrian Saddle* was published in the year of her

[1] Apart from the publication by her of some psychical documents, originally given to her by F. W. H. Myers, under the title 'Some Leaves from the Note Book of a Psychical Enquirer', in the *Occult Review* in 1906.

marriage, and books from her pen appeared at intervals for the rest of her life. Among others, *Things Seen in Palestine* was published in 1913, *Arab in Tent and Town* in 1924, while her final work, *Things Seen in Constantinople*, was published in 1926 when she was nearly seventy. In the light of what we know about her earlier literary activities in psychical research and folklore, any claims implicit in these books that Miss Freer was an authority on the Near East can, I fancy, be regarded as doubtful. It seems probable, indeed, that her writings at this period owed much to her husband.

Her marriage did not amend Miss Freer's disregard for the truth, nor her ability to concoct fantastic stories about herself. In 1977, nine years after the publication of *Strange Things*, the Rev. Donald M. Sinclair of Halifax, Nova Scotia sent to Dr Campbell a handwritten letter (fortunately preserved among family papers) from Miss Freer to his father, the Rev. Maclean Sinclair (d. 1924). The letter and the post-mark on the envelope are both dated 21st February 1906. Miss Freer wrote from Divinity Hall, Meadsville, Pennsylvania, which tells us that for a short time after their marriage Dr Spoer and his wife lived in America. The enthusiasm for Scotland and the name-dropping will not be new to the reader, but Miss Freer's story that she was born in India and had lived in most European countries is worth recording:

Dear Sir,

It is just possible that my name may be known to you in its earlier form of A. Goodrich-Freer, the writer of 'Outer Isles', a friend of Prof. Blackie, Lord Bute, J. W. Carmichael and of Father Allan Macdonald of Eriskay. Otherwise I can only tell you that I am one 'who still in dreams beholds the Hebrides', and who hates Christopher Columbus as I hate a Cawmell!

Professor Cox of Cornell University has sent me your address, as one who may be able to tell me of any Highland Societies in this country—of any journals, magazines or papers? I remember talking of you with that delightful bookseller and writer in Inverness whose name I forget at the moment, I think a Stornaway man—also with Dr Keith Macdonald of Edinbans in Skye. I had thought of putting a letter into the Oban Times which reaches me weekly, to ask what Highlanders are doing this side of the world.

My husband—German by birth—is Professor of Semitic Studies here—we have lately arrived after long travel in the Orient, with a home in Jerusalem. I have lived in most countries in Europe—was born in India, married in Egypt—and never felt an exile and home-sick until I discovered America. Here was no one to whom I

*could say yesterday week 'This is the anniversary of the Massacre
of Glencoe'—nobody ever made dollars out of that!*
Believe me,
Very truly yours,
A. Monica Spoer.

The life of the Spoers was a wandering one. In 1909 Dr Spoer
came to England to study at Lichfield Theological College. Miss
Freer's address in the membership list of the Folklore Society in
1911 was given as 53 Bath Road, Wolverhampton. Her husband was
ordained in that year and went as a chaplain to Cairo, Miss Freer's
address in the records of the Folklore Society in 1912 and 1913 being
Church House, Cairo. Her *Who's Who* entries from 1913 to 1916
give her address as Heliopolis, Egypt, while in the Folklore Society
membership list from 1914 to 1917 she is shown as at Box 104,
Austrian P.O., Jerusalem, which may have been a forwarding address.
In her entry in *Who's Who* in 1925 she said that she had been, from
1918 to 1920, the 'Assistant to Dr Spoer; District Commander
under U.S.A. High Commissioner, Armenia, 1918–19', although
this was not mentioned in the earlier entries from 1918 to 1924. In
the Folklore Society membership list of 1923 she was shown as being
at the American Bible House at Stamboul.

In 1923 Dr Spoer was appointed director of the Foreign Born
American division of the Diocese of Michigan, U.S.A., and he and
his wife went to live in America, Miss Freer's entry in *Who's Who*
for 1925 showing her address as 68 East Hancock Avenue, Detroit,
Michigan. Dr Spoer occupied this position for three years. In 1926
he became the rector of St Peter's Episcopal Church and head of the
English Department at St Albans School at Sycamore, Illinois, and
lived with his wife at St Peter's Rectory in Sycamore. This was the
last address given by Miss Freer in *Who's Who*, but in fact yet
another and final move was made after Dr Spoer had held these
appointments for only one year. In 1927 he became the Chaplain
of the New York Mission Society, and the couple removed to 2540,
30th Road, Astoria, New York. It was from this address that Miss
Freer, fatally ill, was taken to St Luke's Hospital, New York, on
20th December 1930. She lay in hospital for nine weeks waiting for
the end which she knew was inevitable, if we can assume this from
her anxiety in January 1931, some weeks before her death, to ensure
that her 'personal copy' of the *Alleged Haunting of B—— House*
came back to England and the British Museum. She was an elderly
woman of seventy-three, despite her successful claim to be only
fifty-six, and had enjoyed a long and eventful life.

One wonders what ghosts of the past gathered round her bed. Did she think of her brothers in far-away Rutland, the companions of those first beginnings of long ago she had so effectively obliterated, or of the kindly relative who had brought her up in Yorkshire and of whom she had recorded not a single word of appreciation or even of identification? Did she see again the face of the generous and credulous W. T. Stead, the mentor and benefactor of *Borderland* days, whom she had criticized and disowned when it seemed an advantage to do so? Had she a thought for the faithful Constance Moore, whose devoted friendship of over twenty years had provided both a home and daily companionship to the formidable orphan who would otherwise have walked alone? Did she think of Lord Bute, who had believed in her when the spiritualists and psychical re- searchers had united against her, or of the gentle and noble Fr Allan McDonald, whose work of many years she had used? Did she remember the Rev. Charles Shaw, who had supported in print her account of her experiences at Ballechin, and whose hospitality she had rewarded by disillusionment? Or were her last thoughts of the intimacies of those early S.P.R. days with Frederic Myers, her equal, it might be thought, in the exploitation of the kindly and the trustful, and who at the end had deserted and disowned her as she had deserted and disowned others?

She died on 24th February 1931. As has been said, the only obituary of her so far discovered is that which appeared in *Folklore*, in which it was deplored that no biography of a woman of such remarkable and varied achievements had been written.

INDEX OF NAMES, PLACES AND PUBLICATIONS